D1592892

# THE
# LONDON
# ORATORY

### CENTENARY
### 1884-1984

# THE LONDON ORATORY

## CENTENARY
## 1884-1984

EDITED BY MICHAEL NAPIER AND ALISTAIR LAING

TREFOIL

Published by Trefoil Books,
7 Royal Parade, Dawes Road,
London SW6

ISBN 0 86294 045 1 (cloth)
ISBN 0 86294 065 6 (leather)

Set in Bembo by Typecraft (Home Counties) Ltd.,
Bletchley and printed in Hungary

## ACKNOWLEDGEMENTS

The editors are grateful to the Duke of Norfolk and the Greater
London Council for general permission to reproduce photographs
from their archives. In particular they wish to thank the Courtauld
Institute of Art for permission to reproduce plates 76-83, Mr John
Sambrook for plate 41, Mr John F. Brennan for plate 140, and the
Fathers of the Birmingham Oratory for plate 52. A number of the
plates in this volume are taken from the London Oratory album
but of those specially taken the majority are by Prudence Cuming,
and Mr John Donat is responsible for colour plates VI and VII, and
for the black and white plates 16, 55 and 56.

# CONTENTS

# INTRODUCTION

## *Michael Napier*

Henry Edward Manning[1], the Cardinal Archbishop of Westminster, is coming to preach at the solemn dedication of the new church of the Oratory. It is Friday, April 25th, 1884 and more than an hour before the ceremony is due to begin large crowds are besieging the doors; for all tickets of admission have been distributed nearly a week before, and long before eleven every available seat is filled. All catholic England is crowded into the church. The Norfolks are there, the Denbighs, the Lovats, Lord Braye and Lord North. Bedingfeld, Clifford, Dormer, Petre, Blount, Carey Elwes, Eyre, Eyston, Lane Fox, Vaughan, Mathew, and Somers Cocks; all are there; as is Baroness von Hügel and the Spanish Ambassador.

Nothing had been seen like this in London before. The Cardinal was accompanied by sixteen bishops, and some 250 clergy were present. The celebrant of the Mass was Mgr Edward Bagshawe, Bishop of Nottingham, and a former member of the London community; while the choir, augmented to 150 voices, was accompanied by an orchestra of forty performers. For this occasion Cardinal Manning preached one of his most eloquent sermons. 'There are here a multitude of the friends of the Oratory of St Philip. I doubt if there is here anyone that can trace back his memory of friendship with these Fathers as I can. Father Faber, in boyhood, was my school-fellow; in youth he was my friend; and, when we were united in the unity of the Faith, we became brothers together, with a true bond of sympathy that never ceased till his death. ...And now, today, we see what I may call the crown of the work of the Oratory. The Oratory, as a congregation, has long been formed. The place of habitation of the Fathers here, ample and spacious, has been erected, and there was wanting only a church. This magnificent sanctuary is today completed, and for the first time we meet to rejoice with them and for ourselves'.[2]

The great day did not end before a second sermon had been preached in the evening by Father John Morris S.J., Rector of Manresa House. The church was illuminated by large carbon gas burners, but the correspondent of the *Tablet*, from whom this account is drawn, was glad to hear that this was only a temporary arrangement and that it was before long to be 'replaced by the electric light'. After the procession of Our Lady and Benediction of the Blessed Sacrament which concluded the service, 'it was found a matter of no little difficulty to clear the church, crowds lingering to admire the magnificent church and its beautiful altars, and it was not till past eleven that the doors were finally closed'.

The church in which this grand function took place differed in many

*Opposite page:*
1 Cardinal Manning (1808-1892), second Archbishop of Westminster. (*London Oratory album*).

7

respects from what we see today. All was bare and stark, and there was scarcely a touch of gold or colour throughout the building. Although the magnificent Lady Altar was already in place, St Philip's altar was only half completed, and some chapels lacked altars altogether. The High Altar was not the one that stands in the sanctuary now. The exterior lacked its present noble portico and presented a plain brick façade, the congregation entering through a temporary wooden porch. Nor did the familiar dome yet rise above the neighbouring houses. Yet this opening was an event, a significant event. *The Times* felt obliged to notice it in a leading article, if only to warn its readers that, 'this need not be taken as showing any new leaning on the part of England towards the Church of Rome, or as holding out the slightest probability that she would ever return to it', but then went on a shade less stiffly; 'Roman Catholics have nothing to fear from England so long as England has nothing to fear from them'. The report in the *Journal de Rome* on the other hand waxed lyrical. 'Quel spectacle plein de religieuse grandeur et d'immense consolation! Quelle victoire contre l'hérésie enracinée dans ce pays là! Quelle espérance de triomphe pour l'avenir!'

In 1884 the future was looked forward to with hope, and we believe that the hopes of the Fathers and the Catholic community have not been disappointed in the history of the subsequent hundred years. The Oratory has become part of London in a special way, so familiar that it is taken almost for granted. As Mgr Ronald Knox once remarked, 'I have met a taxi-driver who did not know his way to the Athenaeum; nobody has ever met one who did not know his way to the Oratory'.[3] The purpose of this volume is to commemorate the first centenary of the

2 The church in 1893. Gribble's modified design for the portico and facade was carried out 1891-1895, and was completed in time for the St Philip Neri tercentenary celebrations. *(London Oratory album)*.

present church and to offer to the public a collection of essays which, it is hoped, will do something to strip away the mystery which still lurks behind the wall of the Oratory House forecourt. The contributors tell us how the church came to be built, something of the generous benefactors who made its construction and furnishing possible, and how it came to be the settting of some of the most glorious baroque sculpture outside Italy. The hidden treasures of the library and the sacristy are revealed for the first time, while a colourful account is given of the musical tradition for which the London Oratory is so justly famous.

However, the work of an introduction is to introduce, and I must first introduce the *dramatis personae* of this book, the Oratorians themselves. Fortunately there is no need to write in detail about their founder St Philip Neri (1515-1595), nor of Faber (1814-1863) and Newman (1801-1890), nor even of Pope Pius IX (1792-1878), who sent Newman to set up the Oratory in England, and Cardinal Wiseman (1802-1865) who welcomed the first Oratorians to London. All these great and holy men are the subject of recent biographies.[4] Something however must be said of the first companions of Father Faber, whose names appear throughout the following pages. The first Oratory, established in 1849 in converted premises just off the Strand in King William Street, is better described as a chapel than a church. It was only sixty feet by thirty and fifteen feet high, so it is not surprising that it was soon crammed. Wiseman preached at the opening on May 31st. The following year Newman gave

3 Reliquary bust of St Philip Neri, after Alessandro Algardi (1598-1654). Bronze, partially gilt, and crystal. H. 58cm (including socle of 11cm). Dated 1673. Formerly at the Jesi Oratory. *(Private collection).*

4 Pope Pius IX, elected 1846. An anonymous marble bust from early in his pontificate. *(The London Oratory).*

5 Cardinal Wiseman (1802-1865), first Archbishop of Westminster. *(London Oratory album)*.

there his lectures on *The Difficulties of Anglicans,* and W. M. Thackeray and Charlotte Brontë were observed among the congregation. Already however by 1851 the Fathers were dreaming ambitious dreams, 'We must build a good, large and stately church while we are about it. The style must be Italian, and the present idea is to have something on the plan of a basilica, about 200 to 240 feet long, with eventually a stone façade and Corinthian columns'.[5] These dreams were more than realised but they had to wait over thirty years before they came true. The style of King William Street had been Italian from the start, much to the disgust of Pugin and the disappointment of Lord Shrewsbury,[6] who stayed away from the opening. *Romanità* was, and still is, the hallmark of the London Oratorians. The singing of Solemn Vespers on Sunday was introduced from the first at the hour of 3.30 pm, the time which it still retains to this day. When the Fathers moved to their new home in Brompton the Roman siesta was observed, the church closing between 12.30 and 2.30 (although it remained open until 10 pm).[7] An elderly priest remembers as a youth entering the church by pushing aside

6 St Mary's Sydenham. Demolished 1952. *(London Oratory album).*

heavily padded mattresses, popularly known as 'baby crushers', and employed in Roman churches to keep out the heat; where, alas, they are scarcely to be found any longer.[8]

The obvious inadequacy of King William Street and its increasing toll on the health of the community made imperative a move to more salubrious surroundings. In the meantime the Fathers had acquired a country villa at Sydenham,[9] and this was to be their home while the new house at Brompton was going up. The choice of a site so far out worried Newman who thought it 'essentially in a suburb ... a neighbourhood of second-rate gentry and second-rate shops'.[10] He was not to know that in 1853 Charles Henry Harrod would open his grocery store in the Brompton Road. The Fathers did however follow Newman's shrewd advice to build their house first since it would be easier to appeal for a worthy church later, rather than the other way about. The house, with its handsome front elevation, is the one we see today, and was ready for occupation in March 1854. It stands upon the site of old Blemell House, and is commonly compared to an Italian *palazzo*, but surely owes more to Isaac Ware's Chesterfield House (demolished 1937). Externally the temporary church designed by J. J. Scoles (1778-1863) was anything but worthy. It was a long building of yellow brick, built on the site of the kitchen garden. The *Tablet* wrote that it was like, 'one aisle of a huge railway station, and the extreme lowness of the building makes it very ugly indeed'[11]. It was opened on March 22nd and, as is often the way with temporary buildings, stood for twenty-six years. The interior came in time to be richly fitted up and could seat 1200 people. When the time came for its demolition we learn that, 'there were not wanting many

7 Plan of the Blemell House property acquired by the Oratorians in 1852. The Bell and Horns opposite was demolished in 1915 to make way for Empire House. *(London Oratory album)*.

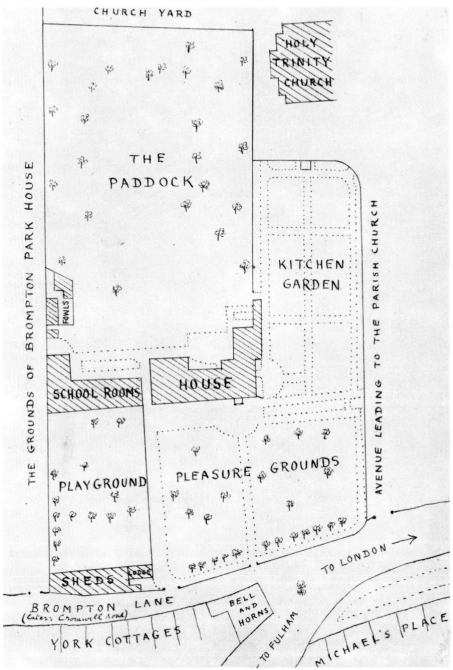

who openly voiced their regrets at its passing'.[12]

In 1879 the new Pope Leo XIII (1810-1903) had created Newman a cardinal, and on May 8th of the following year he came to London to stay for a week at Norfolk House and give public receptions. On Sunday May 9th Newman attended Vespers at the Oratory and gave Benediction, and afterwards preached at the Little Oratory. Father John Norris of the Birmingham Oratory accompanied the cardinal and described the

8 An old photograph of the Oratory House, completed in 1854 to the design of J.J. Scoles. Note the lamp standards and the iron railing round the front lawn. *(London Oratory album)*.

9 The London community in 1877. Back row from left to right: Fr Crewse, Fr C. Bowden, Fr Morris, Fr Gordon, Fr Knox, Fr Stanton (Superior), Fr Rowe, Fr Keogh, Fr S. Bowden, Fr Garnett, Fr Digby Beste. *(London Oratory Album.*

10 Pope Leo XIII. A portrait presented to St Mary's College, Oscott, in 1883 by Monsignor Edmund Stonor (1831-1912), appointed titular Archbishop of Trebizond in 1889. *(The London Oratory).*

11 The staircase of Norfolk House, St James's Square. Designed by Matthew Brettingham in 1748 and demolished in 1938. Drawing by Denis Flanders, 1938. *(Arundel Castle).*

scene. 'I put on his scarlet for him, cappa and all, and then put him into the swell carriage—with hammercloth rugs and two men with sticks behind. I sat in front of him and away we went to the Oratory, to the admiration of the Sunday crowds, such a carriage being an unusual sight on a Sunday.'.[13]

The Duke of Norfolk had arranged for Newman's portrait to be painted by J. E. Millais, and so in 1881 Newman came to London again for the sittings in the artist's studio. This time he stayed not at Norfolk House but at the Oratory, from June 25th until July 6th. On Sunday June 26th he preached in the church. This, and the Benediction of the previous year, would have been in the temporary iron church which was set up in front of the Oratory House, for the last services held in the old church were on the Feast of the Epiphany 1880. By this date work on the new church must have been well advanced. The portrait and the visit were a great success, and Newman presented to the Fathers a set of his works with a graceful inscription.[14]

With the opening of the church in 1884 a new period in the history of the London Oratory had begun. For a hundred years it has been the popular, well-patronised church of London catholics. Monsignor Knox has done well to remind us that, 'the Oratory is not the church of the

Oratorians, It is not *their* church; they are *its priests*. It is their shell, their native element; they glide to and fro unobtrusively in it, looking like those human figures that were put in old prints to show the height of the building'.[15] Within that shell the famous and the humble have mingled together for worship. Sometimes it would be a future Pope,[16] or sometimes a great composer come to enjoy the famous choir. On his last visit to England in 1886 Liszt attended Mass twice at the Oratory. On

12 Felix Kelly. A *capriccio* of the London Oratory, painted *c*.1962. Present whereabouts unknown.

13 A. Chevallier Tayler. *Ecce Agnus Dei,* a *capriccio* of the Oratory Lady Altar (1900). *(Walker Art Gallery, Liverpool).*

I Herbert Gribble's scheme for the decoration of the Oratory (1878). The *baldacchino* over the High Altar was never executed. *(The London Oratory)*.

II The Millais portrait of Cardinal Newman at Arundel Castle, 1881. *(The National Portrait Gallery)*.

the first occasion he heard a Mass of Palestrina, and a week later on April 18th the long Palm Sunday ceremonies made him late for lunch with Baron Orczy.[17]

Some memories of famous preachers ought not to go unrecorded. Monsignor Benson[18] hanging out his drenched shirt from a window at the back of the house after a particularly vigorous sermon; and Father Vincent McNabb[19] striding into the church and straight up the steps of the pulpit in his Dominican habit and hob-nailed boots at literally the last minute, when the agitated Father Superior had given up all for lost.

The building itself has been an inspiration to artists who have indulged themselves in *capricci*. Felix Kelly has lifted the church out of the Brompton Road and has deposited it in a mountainous romantic landscape; while A. Chevallier Tayler[20] has borrowed the Lady Altar (minus the bronze candelabra which were added later from Cardinal Howard's chapel) and placed it in a Gothic church. In the world of art a *capriccio* means the transfer of a familiar object to an unfamiliar setting. May one risk the suggestion that one of the greatest *capricci* of all was the transfer of the Mazzuoli Apostles from their Gothic setting in Siena cathedral. Or do they now look too familiar in their more appropriate home?

I have said that the Oratory has sheltered both the humble and the famous. It has in a special sense been the home of converts. This is particularly true of the Fathers themselves, the great majority of whom have been converts,from the time of the Oxford conversions down to the present.[21] There is a community legend—perhaps *ben trovato*—of the older Fathers sitting in their recreation room after dinner on a Sunday evening, and gently tapping their feet in time to the well-remembered hymn tunes carried across from Evensong in Holy Trinity.

Maurice Baring is only one of the many thousands who have been received at the Oratory. 'On the eve of Candlemas 1909, I was received into the Catholic Church by Father Sebastian Bowden[22] at the Brompton Oratory; the only action in my life which I am quite certain I have never regretted. Father Sebastian began life as an officer in the Scots

*Opposite page:*
14 The Mazzuoli statues in the nave of Siena Cathedral. Photographed before their removal in 1890. *(London Oratory Album).*

15 Father Sebastian Bowden on his cob. *(London Oratory album).*

Guards. He lived all his life at the Oratory and he died in 1920. He was fond, even in old age, of riding about London on a cob. His face was stamped with the victory of character over all other elements. He was a sensible Conservative, a patriot, a fine example of an English gentleman in mind and appearance; a prince of courtesy, and a saint; and I regard my acquaintance with him and the friendship and sympathy he gave me as the greatest privilege bestowed on me by Providence'.[23]

This book does not claim to be in any way a comprehensive history of the last hundred years. It is rather a *Festschrift* for a church. It does not discuss religious opinions. It does not treat of the daily life of the Fathers in their care of the parish entrusted to them as long ago as 1856. Nor does it speak of their work for Catholic education from the Ragged Schools of King William Street days to the London Oratory School and Primary School of our own day. Oratorians are not good at writing about themselves. Their founder taught them to love to be unknown, and they practise an unusual kind of community life where none are bound by vows or promises, and their superior is elected from among

16 The Oratory Church in 1984 after the cleaning of the facade.

themselves every three years. No one has written about the Oratory better than Monsignor Ronald Knox. Not being an Oratorian himself, although extremely familiar with their life,[24] he could write about them in a way which would make an Oratorian blush. Preaching on the occasion of the first hundred years of the Oratory in London, he praised the sense of continuity: 'This sense of continuity depends, not only upon the church itself, but on something in the life, something in the history, perhaps even something in the character, of the priests who serve it. Something in their *life*—the Oratorian does not move about from house to house; ...the priest who received you into the Church, the priest who married you, thirty years ago, if he still lives, still lives in the Brompton Road. ...Something, perhaps, in their *character*; if you are to fit in well with the habits of a community so small, living at such close quarters, you need to be a clubable man; here is no place for doctrinaires and revolutionaries. All that makes for continuity. I do not mean that the Oratory stagnates; it is a hive of industry; but its traditions change slowly, according to the needs of its own nature; they are not imposed on it by the butterfly fashions of the world outside'.

'All these hundred years the Fathers of the Oratory have been at their post; and as each made his last journey to the grave a fresh priest has taken his place, ambitious in his turn to bring the great heart of St Philip into the great heart of London; the old patient attendance to duty, the old gracious courtesy, the old love of music and of pageantry, have never died out'.[25] These words spoken in our church thirty-five years ago are as true today as they were then.

NOTES

1 Manning, a convert and old Harrovian like Faber, succeeded Wiseman as second Archbishop of Westminster. He was created cardinal in 1875. His lying-in-state and Requiem took place in the Oratory in January 1892, when 38,000 mourners filed past the catafalque. Ralph Kerr, *The Oratory in London*, a history published in instalments in the Oratory Parish Magazine (1921-1932) February 1929.

2 Printed in full in the *Tablet*, 3 May 1884. Manning, like Wiseman, had been a Brother of the Little Oratory in Rome.

3 From *The Oratorians in London*, a sermon preached at the Oratory, 6 June 1949 to commemorate the centenary of the Oratorians in London. Published in *Occasional Sermons* of Ronald A. Knox, ed. Philip Caraman S.J., Burns & Oates, 1960, p. 283.

4 Meriol Trevor, *Apostle of Rome: a Life of Philip Neri*, Macmillan, 1966; Ronald Chapman, *Father Faber*, Burns & Oates, 1961; Meriol Trevor, *Newman: The Pillar and the Cloud* and *Newman: Light in Winter*, Macmillan, 1962; E. E. Y. Hales, *Pio Nono*, Eyre & Spottiswoode, 1954; Brian Fothergill, *Nicholas Wiseman*, Faber & Faber, 1963.

5 Kerr, *op. cit.*, O.P.M. November, 1926.

6 John Talbot, 16th Earl of Shrewsbury (1791-1852), the patron of Pugin, and the first benefactor of both Faber and Newman.

7 H. S. Bowden, *Guide to the Oratory*, 1912 edn.

8 Monsignor A. N. Gilbey, born 1901.

9 The land had been given by Mrs Bowden, and St Mary's, as it was called, was built in 1852. Almost exactly a hundred years later it was sold to the local council under threat of compulsory purchase. Faber indulged there his taste for gardening, and laid out the cemetery. 'You will long for your nine feet of it', he wrote, 'when you see its pensive cypresses and its holy calm'. Kerr, *op. cit.*, O.P.M. December, 1923.

10  Letter from Newman to Faber of 18 September 1852. Printed in Vol. XV of *The Letters and Diaries of John Henry Newman*.

11  The *Tablet*, 17 December 1853.

12  Kerr, *op. cit., O.P.M.*, April 1927.

13  Meriol Trevor, *Newman: Light in Winter*, p. 584.

14  *Ibid.* pp. 588-589.

15  Ronald A. Knox, *op. cit., p. 282.*

16  Both Mgr Pacelli (Pius XII) and Mgr Montini (Paul VI) worshipped at the Oratory when visiting England.

17  The first reference to the Oratory is in a letter to the Princess Carolyne von Sayn-Wittgenstein. Writing on April 16th he reports, 'His Eminence Cardinal Manning received me most kindly. That shows you that here no more than in Hungary am I in disgrace with the Catholic authorities'. The second reference is contained in Constance Bache's book 'Brother Musicians' (1901). Constance Bache adored the musical genius of Liszt and kept a diary of events during the course of the visit. I am grateful to Mr Edward de Rivera for providing me with this information.

18  Robert Hugh Benson (1871-1914), convert son of Edward White Benson, Archbishop of Canterbury, and younger brother of E. F. Benson and A. C. Benson. Author of numerous 'catholic' novels, now ripe for reappraisal.

19  Vincent McNabb O.P. (1868-1943), noted preacher and poet, closely associated with Hilaire Belloc and G. K. Chesterton.

20  Albert Chevallier Tayler (1862-1925), a convert to Catholicism. Well known as a genre painter and portrait artist, who exhibited at the Royal Academy from 1884. His portraits of Admiral Earl Beatty and Field Marshall Earl Haig are in the Guildhall Art Gallery.

21  At the time of writing (1984), out of a community of eleven, nine are converts, as are also the two novices.

22  In 1878 Father Bowden nearly received the young Oscar Wilde into the Church, but when the day came for his reception there arrived at the Oratory, instead of a determined catechumen, a large box of lilies. Wilde was not to enter the Church until the day before his death in 1900. See André Raffalovich's article in *Blackfriars*, Vol. VIII, no. 92, 1927.

23  Maurice Baring, *The Puppet Show of Memory*, 1922, pp. 395-96.

24  After his conversion, Ronald Knox lived at the Oratory as a lodger for thirteen months, 1917-18. Evelyn Waugh, *The Life of Ronald Knox*, p. 168.

25  Ronald A. Knox, *The Oratorians in London, op. cit.*, pp. 284-85.

# THE ARCHITECTURE OF THE LONDON ORATORY CHURCHES

## *Roderick O'Donnell*

The great Catholic historian and liturgical scholar Edmund Bishop wrote from Rome in 1895 to the Oratorian Fr Antrobus comparing the new Oratory church with two great churches of Baroque Rome, the Gesù and the Chiesa Nuova: 'I do not think that they are to be compared to the London Oratory ...I laugh at these Roman wonders ...and this ...brings to my mind that perhaps the nineteenth century is not so absurdly behindhand in these matters as we are apt to fancy—that those who come after us may perhaps think a little better of us than we have thought ourselves.'[1] The centenary guide to the third London Oratory church is appropriately the place where 'those who come after us' can begin the re-assessment which Bishop, to his very bones a mediaevalist, foresaw.[2]

This essay investigates the architectural and liturgical life of the Oratory from its foundation in 1849 until the end of the century, with special emphasis on the present church consecrated in 1884, its protagonists in the Oratorian community, its architect, the competition held in 1878, the sources of the design, the building of the church, its financing, and its patrons. The wider background of the Gothic Revival and mid-nineteenth century Ultramontanism and liturgical development will also be mentioned.

The present Oratory church, built between 1880 and 1884, is the second on this site, and the third since the Oratory was established in London, in 1849. As a large and prominently placed classical church it is of considerable importance in English architectural history of the period, proclaiming as it did the arrival in late Victorian ecclesiastical London of the hitherto neglected Renaissance and Baroque styles. Its architect, Herbert Gribble (1847-1894), wrote: 'those who had no opportunity of going to Italy to see an Italian church had only to come here to see the model of one.'[3] His church, as something foreign, exotic and Italian, coincided with a popular view of Catholicism, partly fostered by the Oratory itself, which allowed the Archbishop of Canterbury to dismiss the Catholic Church in England as 'the new Italian mission.'[4] Yet the classical style of the Oratory was singular even in Catholic terms. For the previous two generations Catholic churches, like those of the Church of England, had been exclusively Gothic. This extraordinary pervasiveness of the Gothic Revival was undoubtedly due to the influence of the convert Catholic architect A. W. Pugin (1812-1852), whose role within the Catholic church was first successfully challenged by the nascent Oratory, firstly in the Midlands and later in London.

The Oratory was always remarkable for its Italian rather than Gothic dress, from the Lowther Rooms off the Strand fitted up as a temporary church in 1849, through the first church on this site (1853-4), to the existing building. Even in Catholic circles this adherence to classicism throughout the heyday of the Gothic Revival was almost unique: although both would have preferred the classical, Cardinal Manning in 1868 and Cardinal Vaughan in 1894 found themselves presiding over a Gothic and an 'Italo-Byzantine' scheme for Westminster Cathedral respectively. The choice of a Baroque design for the present church, the outcome of a competition which specified as the style: 'that of the Italian Renaissance', was to have something of a liberating influence on late Victorian and Edwardian church design. Where the first two Oratory churches overcame Pugin's liturgical dictatorship within the Catholic church was by qualifying without upsetting the stylistic hegemony of the Gothic Revival, the present church went further in overcoming the reluctance, not only of Catholic, but also of other architects who can be identified as Catholics in the competition built classical churches shortly afterwards.[5] The Oratory also stands out as extraordinarily early in its return to Renaissance classical themes,[6] when compared to contemporary Continental church architecture. The first Anglican classical church for half a century in London followed in 1887-8, also by an Oratory competitor.[7]

The future Monsignor Ronald Knox, a recent if celebrated convert, wrote in 1918 of: 'Catholics accustomed to worship at Downside or at the Oratory indifferently'[8]—implying a stylistic insensitivity in contrast to the highly volatile tastes of fashionable Anglicanism which he left behind him. Knox however would have been quite wrong to suppose that such indifference to style existed in 1874, when the decision was taken to build the present church, or in 1849 when the Oratory arrived in London. The Oratorian presentation of the liturgy as Continental and Italianate was highly controversial in mid- and late Victorian England. It challenged the association of religion with the Middle Ages, an almost universal Romantic response after 1800 both in Britain and on the Continent, which was given particular edge for Catholics and others by Pugin. For the mid-Victorians it was axiomatic that church architecture should be Gothic, a belief disseminated as widely within the Anglican, and later the Nonconformist Churches, as it was initially by Pugin amongst Catholics.

Pugin's architectural, historical and moral critique identified the classical style, whether Antique, Renaissance or Regency, with 'Paganism'. The 'Pagan' style was clearly inappropriate for Christian churches, and indeed Pugin soon came to talk of the Gothic as the 'Christian' style, to the exclusion of all others. Pugin first identified the introduction of classicism into England with the Protestant Reformation, but he moved on to associate it with the Catholic Church of the Counter-Reformation and the *Ancien Régime*. Contemporary Continental Catholicism, so full of fascination even for such Anglicans as the young Frederick Faber, Vicar of Elton in Huntingdonshire, was for Pugin a series of liturgical disappointments.[9]

The struggle between Pugin and his opponents, largely consisting of the Oratorians and their supporters in the Catholic press, is known as the 'Rood Screen Controversy'. Pugin found his architectural and liturgical standards overturned by the much-publicised temporary Oratory churches. Although both were classical, it was not this eccentric stylistic choice, but the different liturgical and church-planning ideals of the Oratory which were to be enormously influential. It would not be an exaggeration to say that the Oratorian concept of a parish or congregational liturgy was to predominate from 1850 until the end of the century and later.

The Oratorians were mostly converts who had followed either Newman or Faber into the Church. Paradoxically, they had already had their fill of Pugin's teachings through his Anglican admirers in the Senior and Junior Common Rooms of Oxford and Cambridge. As converts they wished to forget Gothic Oxford, and the obvious reaction was to turn to Classical Rome. Pugin, anticipating the secession of the 'glorious Oxford men' in 1841, saw them as allies in the Gothic Revival; now he wrote: 'no men have been as disappointing as these'; and of the Oratory: 'I give the whole Order up for ever.'[10]

The argument between Pugin and the Oratory was primarily liturgical. Pugin insisted on the adoption not only of the Gothic style, but also of the additive, sub-divided church plan of the late Middle Ages. For Pugin the mystery of the Mass and the liturgy required yet further shrouding within the furnishings and arrangement of his churches. No church was complete without its Rood Screen dividing the church from the sanctuary, where behind the closed doors one might glimpse something of the Mass through open-work Gothic tracery. Pugin burst into tears or threatened to resign a commission when the screen was questioned.

The converted Lowther Rooms were arranged on exactly opposite lines: 'well may they cry out against screens ...I always said they wanted rooms, not churches, and now they have got them.'[11] As Newman pointed out, the Oratory was a Counter-Reformation not a pre-Reformation Order, and thus the Gothic was for it an anachronism: 'Now is it wonderful that I prefer St Philip to Mr Pugin?'[12] For Newman and Faber Continental Catholicism was an ideal, not, as for Pugin, a decline. Even as Anglicans they had returned from Italy full of credulous enthusiasm for its religion and religiosity, which as Catholics they eagerly imitated, even down to an Italian pronunciation of Latin. If, like Pugin and the Goths, they accepted the importance of a Latin liturgy governed by the strictest rubrical and ceremonial elaboration, they saw it in Italian, not Gothic, dress, Such a liturgy, particularly with its emphasis on Benediction, called for an approach quite different to Pugin's. Newman wrote of Pugin's new church at Fulham: 'his altars are so small you can't have a Pontifical High Mass at them, his tabernacles so low that you can scarce have an Exposition, his East windows so large that everything is hidden in the glare, and his screens so heavy that you might as well have the function in the sacristy, for all the seeing of it by the congregation.'[13]

Although the Italian style of the Strand Oratory carried with it an important message for Victorian Catholics, the Oratory was very much more than a church with unusual decoration. For Faber it was his 'Spiritual Mechanics Institute', with the clerks, shop assistants, and 'lawyers, medical students, etc., pouring pell-mell into the Church' every night.[14] Pugin, taking up the same point, exclaimed: 'What degradation for religion. Why it is worse than the Socialists …Sad times, I cannot imagine what the world will come to if it goes on much longer.'[15] While the Earl of Arundel, the future Duke of Norfolk, knelt on bare boards to hear Faber's first Mass in the new house, the Earl of Shrewsbury, Pugin's munificent patron in the Midlands, refused to contribute. By contrast, Cardinal Wiseman found here a church much closer to his taste than Pugin's Southwark Cathedral, his church from 1848 to 1850. Wiseman not only attended the opening in 1849, but on St Philip's Day 1851 preached a sermon which the *Tablet* took as: 'The pronouncement of the Cardinal, evidently called forth by the recent tirades of the ultragoths' in the Rood Screen Controversy.[16] For Newman, it was the crowded church where he delivered his 'Lectures on certain difficulties felt by Anglicans in submitting to the Catholic Church.'[17] The second church at Brompton (1853-4) was even more intimately the scene of Faber's preaching and spiritual direction, issued as eight volumes in as many years, beginning with *All for Jesus* in 1853. On the edge of Hyde Park, it became particularly the church of fashion and of converts. The *Tablet* thought the new church 'will be in easy reach of the "far advanced" Anglicans in the neighbourhood of Knightsbridge and Chelsea',[18] that is of High Church Anglicans ripe for conversion. For *Punch* it was a source of endless malicious jokes.

The present church (1880-1884) was to be the memorial to Faber, in Manning's words: 'That eloquent and sweet voice …that mind, more fertile than any I have known, …that tongue facile and fluent …a priest and a pastor, a guide and spiritual writer, whose words convinced not only reason, but moved the hearts of men.'[19] Newman, who refused invitations even from the Duke of Norfolk to attend the opening, somewhat petulantly wrote of the new church as: 'A building on so grand a scale …as of disadvantage to us' (in the Birmingham Oratory).[20] The new church remained musically and liturgically faithful to the traditions of Newman's and Faber's day, improving as we shall see on its importance in London. The new Oratory was Manning's, and later Vaughan's, unofficial Cathedral.[21]

Today the Oratory is not only a busy South Kensington parish church, but a church uniquely loyal to its liturgical tradition going back to 1849, a remarkable achievement in the years of bewildering liturgical change which have followed the Second Vatican Council. Today the Oratory fulfills a spiritual role as distinctive as that of the 1850s or 1880s—in countering, not the liturgical orthodoxies of the Gothic Revival, but of a reform which has unintentionally allowed an *ad hoc* vernacularism to replace a ritual Latin liturgy. At the Oratory the reformed liturgy is performed in the official language of the Church, and with all the ceremonial and musical splendour permitted in the current rubrics, but often omitted elsewhere.

*Ultramontanism*

To Victorian Catholics the influence of Faber was more apparent than that of Newman, a paradox only partly explained by the current misapprehension of Newman as a patron saint of ecumenical reconciliation between the Church of England and Rome. The new church was to embody Faber's deeply-held belief in a Roman and papalist interpretation of Catholicism, in the face of opposition not only from Pugin, but from contemporary Protestantism and liberalism. The identification with not only the office, but the person, of the Pope was particularly the achievement of a papacy threatened by the French Revolution, nationalism and liberalism. The climax came in the reign of Pius IX (1846-1878), which began with flight and exile in 1848, and ended with his confinement as 'Prisoner of the Vatican' in 1870 after the loss of the Papal States and the occupation of Rome itself. The worse the reverses the Pope suffered, the more Catholic Europe rallied to his cause. The Pope answered with statements condemning the cherished nineteenth century shibboleths on liberalism, progress and the rest, and more lastingly exalting the claims of the Papacy with the dogmatic definition of Papal Infallibility (1870).

Wiseman's Hymn *Full in the panting heart of Rome*, sung without blushing by Catholic congregations until twenty years ago, provides a

17 Pope Pius IX. A marble relief signed L. Bartolini 1847, the year after the Pope's election. *(The London Oratory)*.

18 The Oratory processional madonna. 'Processions with banners and images...all that makes a Catholic Feast...as completely and simply as in a Catholic country'.

graphic word-picture of the Ultramontane movement beginning under:

The golden roof, the marble walls
The Vatican's majestic halls ...it sweeps beyond the solemn plain
Peals o'er the Alps, across the main ...From torrid south to frozen north
The wave harmonious stretches forth
Yet strikes no chord more true to Rome's
Than rings within our hearts and homes
God Bless our Pope, the great, the good.

If nowadays unspoken, the sentiment survives to some extent, in spite of the Second Vatican Council, in the adulation accorded to Pope John Paul II. Faber commemorated the Pope's troubles in 1848 with a hymn:

O Mary, Mother Mary! Our tears are flowing fast
For Mighty Rome, St Philip's home, is desolate and waste
There are wild beasts in her palaces far fiercer and more bold
Than those that licked the martyrs' feet in heathen days of Old.[23]

His *O purest of Creatures* was written for the Strand Church at the height of the 'Papal aggression' agitation, after the Pope's restoration of the English Catholic hierarchy; *Sweet Saviour bless us ere we go* was the evening service hymn, and *Faith of Our Fathers* had appropriately varied words for England and Ireland respectively.[24] Faber acknowledged his debt to the Protestant evangelical and revivalist tradition, whereas Pugin denounced 'The doggerel rhymes and poetic effusions of a few individuals whose tendencies and principles should have led them to Geneva, but who appear to have mistaken their road and found their way into the Catholic Church ...(who) use the ancient liturgy as a mere vehicle for the display of their Methodism.'[25]

Faber's 'Popular services' continued at Brompton, particularly in the services of the Confraternities of St Patrick—to encourage the Irish to frequent Mass and Holy Communion—and of the Precious Blood, which attracted 'on average two thousand persons' to the weekly Sunday evening service in 1893, as well as thirty-eight thousand members throughout the country by 1869.[26]

Fr Sebastian Bowden, writing of the church in the same year, contrasted 'the dull and dismal streets of our great city and its begrimed, driven and melancholy population, with nothing to raise their spirits but a *bank holiday*, with a feast-day inside the church: 'Processions with banners and images, confraternities in their habits, festoons and lights innumerable, orchestral and popular music—all that makes a Catholic Feast ...as completely and simply as in a Catholic country.'[27]

Apart from the debt to Geneva, Faber's pastoral method drew heavily on Catholic Europe, particularly on the revivalist mission-giving of St Alphonsus Liguori and the Redemptorists. Faber gave dramatic missions to the Irish, appealing to a stony audience: ' "How can I touch your hearts? I have prayed to Jesus, I have prayed to Mary; whom shall I pray to next?"; continuing on his knees: "I will pray to *you* dear Irish children to have mercy on your own souls"; the whole congregation fell on their knees, and for some minutes nothing was heard but their sobs and prayers.'[28] Missions were one of the many continental Catholic practices which spread through the Church in England at this time. We find that Stations of the Cross were set up for the first time in 1854, and were perfomed every Friday; by 1893 these were 'one of the most popular devotions in the church', held each Friday evening.[29] Equally characteristic were the dedications of side chapels—to the Sacred Heart of Jesus, and to St Joseph (to Pugin's followers, both 'modern' devotions), and less controversially, to Our Lady.[30]

The most 'modern' development at the Oratory was the emphasis on the worship of the Blessed Sacrament outside the Mass. Charles Reding, the hero of Newman's novel *Loss and Gain* (1848) was converted, not by High Mass in a Gothic cathedral, but by Benediction in an unfinished brick church.[31] In 1849 the Oratory held Rosary, sermon and Benediction on Sundays in addition to the appropriate liturgical office, Vespers, together with a further Benediction on Thursdays. In 1850 Benediction was given on holy days of obligation, on days of devotion, on all feasts of Our Lord and Our Lady; and by 1893 on Sundays, holy days, Thursdays, Saturdays and daily in May and October.[32] The *Quarant'Ore*, or Forty hours devotion, was also held as part of the cycle begun in each church by Wiseman in Lent 1849, but has been allowed to lapse in the rest of the Westminster diocese. The Oratory *Quarant'Ore* was always of special splendour, and is still held every Lent, in line with Pope John Paul II's letter on devotion to the Blessed Sacrament, *Inestimabile Donum* (1980). It was the holding of the first ever *Quarant'Ore* in London in 1848 that sparked off the Rood Screen Controversy. The generically Italianate tendency of such a liturgy may be noted. While some complained that:

19 The sanctuary decorated for the Quarant'ore or forty hours devotion. Introduced in London by Wiseman in 1849, this devotion is still maintained at the Oratory each year during the fourth week of Lent. *(London Oratory album)*.

'We may be Catholics, but need not be so completely and absolutely *Roman* Catholics as to introduce all the latest ultra-Italian innovations',[33] the Oratory party smelt crypto-Anglicanism in this reaction, and prescribed yet more *Romanità*. An informed Anglican observer noted the important shift in Catholic liturgical practice, and traced it to Newman's revolutionary *Essay on the Development of Christian Doctrine* (1845): 'The Oratorians under Mr Newman and Mr Faber have approved the doctrine of development of dogma ...Oratorian Ecclesiology is that the appreciation of the Real Presence ...exists now as it has never existed before ...The Oratorians talk of Benediction, as, next to the Mass, the service ...to the neglect of Vespers.'[34] The Pugin party was by contrast much more 'liturgical', with its emphasis on plain-chant and the Divine Office as the staples of a congregational liturgy.

*The New Church*

The first church on the present site (plate 21) was a temporary brick structure, along the lines suggested during the Controversy as an antidote to Pugin's supposedly expensive churches. The original contract was for a mere £1800, but the new Metropolitan Building Act (1853) raised the necessary costs to £2400.[35] Although there were rumours that a £50,000 church was to be built, the Fathers had no such intentions. Like Newman in Birmingham, they built a substantial Italianate house, with the 14th Duke of Norfolk paying for the wing containing the Little Oratory with the Library above, the arrangement at the Chiesa Nuova.[36] The architect of all these was John Joseph Scoles, whose London

20 The sanctuary of the 1854 church in its final form. The altar rails, choir stalls and the sanctuary flooring, the gift of the Duchess of Argyll in 1856, were retained in the present church. *(London Oratory Album)*.

Catholic churches included Our Lady, Lisson Grove (1833–1836, much altered since) and St John, Duncan Terrace, Islington (1841–1843). Although enlarged and lavishly refurnished, the temporary church seemed inadequate to the second generation of Oratorians and such friends as the 15th Duke of Norfolk. The decision to build a new church was taken in celebration of the half-jubilee of the London Congregation in 1874. Three figures of importance emerge from this process: Fr Keogh, superior from 1877 to 1880; the architect Herbert Gribble; and Henry, 15th Duke of Norfolk, whose promise of £20,000 allowed the Fathers to address themselves immediately to the design of the church rather than to the tedious business of fund-raising.[37]

The author of the important history of the Oratory published in the *Oratory Parish Magazine* saw Fr Keogh as the prime mover behind the new church. Stephen Keogh (1833–1887) interestingly embodies the

21 The 1854 temporary church and the more substantial house, both by J.J. Scoles. *(London Oratory album).*

22 Plan of the 1854 church in its final form after many side-chapels had been added. *(London Oratory album).*

23 Father Stephen Keogh. He bought by subscription the Lady Altar in the present church. *(London Oratory album).*

24 Father Philip Gordon. He was six times elected Superior of the London Community. *(London Oratory album).*

25 Father Sebastian Bowden, nephew of Mrs Elizabeth Bowden. He paid for the decoration of the Little Oratory in 1872 by J. Hungerford Pollen. *(London Oratory album).*

solution to the rivalry between the convert 'Oxford men' and the mis-leadingly titled 'old Catholics'—a problem that had confronted Pugin and Newman's followers respectively. The older tradition is suggested by his Irish name and by his education at St Edmund's College, Ware, then the London District seminary. Yet at St Edmund's he had been the favourite pupil of the Ultramontane convert and theologian, W. G. Ward; and when he joined the Oratory, he wrote a pamphlet in 1870 opposing the subsequently excommunicated Liberal Catholic Döllinger at the Vatican Council.[38] Keogh with two other future Superiors, Fr Philip Gordon (1827-1900) and Fr Sebastian Bowden (1836-1920), sat on the new church committee from 1874; and as Superior from 1877, saw the new church through the architectural competition (1878), the appointment of Gribble, and the beginning of the church according to the revised designs of 1879 and 1880. There had been a connection between Keogh and Gribble as early as 1874, and we may be sure that he was behind the selection of Gribble's competition design by eight votes to five.[39] The purchase of the Lady Altar and the subscription for its erection in 1883 was equally Keogh's idea.[40]

Herbert Gribble was an otherwise obscure Plymouth architect, whose *chef d'oeuvre* is undoubtedly the Oratory. Apart from a similar design for a Jesuit church at Poona in India, his church work was routinely Gothic Revival. The achievement of so mature a classical church thus appears at variance not only with contemporary church architecture, but even with Gribble's own career.[41] Where then did he learn his classicism? Amongst contemporary Catholic church architects in London, only George Goldie had designed a classical church, the domed cruciform SS John & Elizabeth Hospital Chapel (1865), richly marbled, and furnished with imported antique furnishings. Scoles's temporary Oratory church also introduced some important decorative themes, particularly all-over internal polychromy.

There was a more important link with the adjacent National Art-Training School of the Science and Art Department, within what is now the Victoria and Albert Museum. Here, the Instructor in Decorative Art, F. W. Moody, and others, instilled a richly-decorated round-arched classical style, drawn from historically eclectic sources. This partly coincided with the anti-Gothic Revival stance of the historian and architectural theorist, James Fergusson. It was, quite extraordinarily, to Moody and Fergusson, rather than to a practising Catholic architect, that the Fathers turned for their first two designs in 1875.

The intervention of Fergusson was especially appropriate. In 1850 he had begun an exchange with Pugin and others in the *Builder*, denouncing the Gothic Revival as 'copyism'—a phrase immediately taken up in the Rood Screen Controversy. As a historian, Fergusson was dismissive of the 'archaeological' method of the Gothic Revival: 'Archaeology is not architecture ...but a science'[42]; suggesting instead a style derived from that of the Italian Early and High Renaissance.

Although the 'Fergusson-Moody' design settled the plan as that of a nave flanked by side-chapels, with an apsed sanctuary flanked by a sacristy and further main side-chapel, it was stylistically far from what the Fathers were seeking.[43] Moody's decorative style may be seen in the Museum, particularly in the lavish ceramic, or west, staircase; whilst Fergusson's distance from the visual image of a new church held by the Fathers emerges from his condemnation of the entire tradition of Renaissance and Baroque church-planning deriving from Leone Battista Alberti's S Andrea in Mantua (1472-1512): 'S Andrea ...has been reproduced some hundreds of times on all scales, from that of St Peter's in Rome to that of the smallest village church ...and the result is that no progress has been made, so that at the present hour the Italians are just where they were three centuries ago ...it must be confessed that considering their opportunities, the result is on the whole negative and unsatisfactory.'[44] Gribble's church would in Fergusson's view reflect its sources too closely, as we shall see after investigating the competition.

*The Competition*

Before dealing with the competition, it is important to establish Gribble's previous links with the Oratory. He was known to Fr Keogh in 1874, he was a convert of the Fathers, and he was assistant in the well-known Catholic architectural practice of Joseph Aloysius Hansom. The latter had been concerned with additions to the Little Oratory block in 1872-3, and was also architect of the neighbouring Servite church, Fulham Road (1874-1875), and architect of the Duke of Norfolk's church of St Philip Neri, Arundel (1868-1873). Gribble was also closely associated with the Duke's highly involved claims over Arundel parish church.[45]

The architectural competition played an important part in the development of the architectural profession in England in the nineteenth century, and it occasionally brought unknown architects such as Gribble to prominence. Amongst Catholic clergy and patrons, however, competitions were not much favoured: Pugin resisted them, and J. F. Bentley shunned them, but was providentially awarded Westminster

26 Herbert Augustine Gribble, architect of the present church, built between 1880 and 1884. *(London Oratory album).*

Cathedral when Cardinal Vaughan realised this.[46] The Fathers originally thought of restricting the competition to Catholics, but its terms were open when it was announced in January 1878.[47]

The competition has been investigated fully in the *Survey of London, Vol. XLI: Southern Kensington; Brompton.*[48] Our concern is with Gribble's role. Clearly he was already near the centre of the debate amongst the Fathers on a new church design, at a time when 'there were almost as many plans as there were Fathers'.[49] His success consisted in creating a convincing visual resolution of the conflicting ideas of the Fathers, with a design published in the *Building News* in March 1876— that is, three months after the rejection of the Fergusson-Moody second scheme.[50] In this sense, it seems that the competition was held to set Gribble's design in context, rather than to select an architect. Equally decisive was the failure of the competition's *Instructions to Architects* to specify financial limitations, which left the assessor, the distinguished architect Alfred Waterhouse, at a serious disadvantage. There were as usual many complaints arising out of the competition, and the much-disappointed Henry Clutton, a convert and relative of Manning's, declined to accept the second prize awarded to him.

Such controversies were commonplace, however. More important for us is the light the competition sheds on contemporary Catholic architecture. Of the thirty schemes submitted, as many as ten can be identified as by Catholics, and of these nine were amongst the twelve selected by Waterhouse. These were by Adams and Kelly of Leeds and London; Henry Clutton, Dunn and Hansom of Newcastle (omitted by Waterhouse), Gribble himself, G. G. Scott, junior (converted subsequently, in 1880), Bernard Smith of Hull, Francis Tasker and Bonella, J. J. Walford, Albert Vicars of London and John O'Neill of O'Neill and Byrne, Dublin. Six of these architects were shortly to design classical churches, some of them in London—a striking example of the already noted effect of the competition. A non-Catholic submission of particular exoticism was that of George Nattress, although not noticed by Waterhouse.[51]

*Architectural sources of the new Church*

Gribble's church made a number of genuflections both to English and European Renaissance and Baroque church architecture, or as he put it, to the 'Italian church ...model.' His sources were those disparaged by Fergusson: S Andrea, Mantua and the Gesù (begun in 1568)—the two great models of Baroque Catholic church planning. At S Andrea, Alberti substituted side-chapels set at right-angles to the nave for the established basilican church-plan of a nave with parallel aisles. He also hit upon the marriage of the longitudinal with the central plan which was to become standard to Renaissance church-planning, in the form of a crossing-dome presiding over sanctuary and transepts of equal projection, with a longer nave. Gribble also took from Alberti his internal nave elevation, consisting of a giant order applied to solid piers, with a minor order articulating the arched openings in between. This triumphal-arch motif established a rhythmic alternation between open and closed along the

the Oratory Church Brompton.

HC.

III  The Oratory Church, Brompton, by Sir Hugh Casson, 1984.

IV The singing of Vespers in the King William Street Chapel c.1850. The statue of Our Lady of Victories is that on the Lady Altar in the present church. (*The London Oratory*).

RESPICE STELLAM VOCA MARIAM

nave. From the Gesù, Gribble took the secondary axis parallel to the nave formed by the connections between the side-chapels. Waterhouse, himself a planner of distinction, commented on this when he commended: 'the openings and the accessibility of the side-chapels; the admirably continued passage round the church for processions and for gaining access to different parts of the church when the nave is crowded.'[52]

Neither Alberti nor Vignola was faced with the problem of insufficient Northern light. Instead of their deep-footed tunnel vaults, Gribble created separate vaults over each bay, with a succession of small glazed cupolas rising out of the middle of each vault: three over the nave and one over the sanctuary. The vaults over the first and last bays of the nave are groined cross-vaults; those over the middle bay of the nave and the sanctuary are saucer domes supported by diadem arches, with large clerestory windows, like Wren's over St Paul's. Gribble, with his iron and glass cupolas, had the advantage over Wren, and Pevsner somewhat archly noted them as: 'the only distinctly modern and northern idea' in the church. The vaults over each bay are separated by broad coffered arches, which continue the rythm of the double pilasters of the nave elevation, as at St Paul's. The crossing-dome, which Gribble strove hard to include in the first building campaign of 1880-1884, is a shallow inner shell springing directly from the four crossing piers, lit by eight oculi between the ribs and, originally, by the central oculus. Gribble thus not only solved the problem of lighting the church, but by rejecting a continuous tunnel vault in favour of alternating vaults over each bay, gave added variety and height to the church, and reduced the funnel-like perspective effect of his models. Gribble's main entablature is likewise broken forward over the double pilasters and crossing piers, thus avoiding an insistent visual thrust towards the east end.

Whereas many competitors, such as Henry Clutton, interpreted the competition rubric of 'Italian Renaissance' as what we should now call High Renaissance or Mannerist, Gribble himself looked to the Baroque, although not to a Baroque as advanced as that of Bernini or Borromini. Gribble thus made important advances with his introduction of allusions to the Baroque, which we tend to associate with the public architecture of the Edwardian period. This is particularly true of the exterior elevations with their channelled rustication, a reference both to Wren and to French seventeenth and eighteenth century classicism, that prompted the aphorism that Gribble's competition design was: 'a réchauffé of St Paul's, the Lowther Arcade and Newgate.'[54] The façade was to have two *campanili,* the bases of which cleverly mask the junction of the nave and side-chapels, with between them a columnar screen providing a deep porch, another essential Northern requirement. Without the upper storeys of the towers, the Baroque thrust of the elevation depends on the heightened silhouette of the lead-covered outer dome added in 1895 by the Catholic architect George Sherrin.[55]

*The building of the new church 1880-1884*

Although Gribble's design was recommended by Waterhouse and accepted by the Fathers, there was clearly less confidence in Gribble's practical qualifications for carrying out so ambitious a building. It was unanimously voted: 'that the accepted design be carried out by the author in conjunction with another architect.'[56] Four Catholics—Clutton, Goldie, Charles Alban Buckler (not a competitor) and the obscure Edward Walford— were suggested, and the latter was appointed. In 1882 however, Gribble was awarded sole charge of the works: 'the Congregation having ample proof of Mr Gribble's professional ability and great devotion to their interests.'[57]

The 1878 competition design was reworked by Gribble, with such important consequences as those of building in ashlar with Portland stone rather than in brick, constructing the vaults and domes of concrete, and cladding the columns and pilasters with Plymouth marble. Gribble also designed and built the temporary iron church. The foundation stone of the new church was laid in June 1880, but not by Newman, who declined the honour. The main contract—omitting the façade, *campanili* and the double domes—was awarded to the builder George Shaw, of Westminster. The walls were finished in March 1882, the roof and inner dome in March 1883; the church was consecrated on April 16th 1884, and opened on April 25th.[58]

*Finance and Patronage*

The new church was an extremely expensive building. The competition specified no limitations on cost, so that the estimates for the entries fluctuated somewhat wildly between £35,000 and £200,000. Gribble estimated his scheme at between £35,000 and £70,000, Waterhouse at £91,775; £93,302 had been spent by the end of 1885.[59] The majority of this sum was given by pious individuals. Throughout the nineteenth century, the purchase of sites and the building of schools and churches imposed almost insupportable burdens on Catholic missions. This was especially true in towns, and in the absence of rich donors such as Pugin's patron, the Earl of Shrewsbury. In London between 1815 and 1835 the number of Catholic missions remained constant, and only three new churches were built; despite an increase of at least half in the Catholic population, only seventeen churches were opened between 1840 and 1850.[60] The *Rambler* in 1850 estimated that Catholic London required twenty-five new churches, yet under Cardinal Manning only three new large secular churches were built north of the Thames between 1863 and 1892, so that the Westminster Diocese is not conspicuous for its church architecture in the High Victorian period.[61]

One of the arguments of the Rood Screen Controversy concerned the choice supposed to exist between cheap temporary churches and expensive permanent buildings. For Pugin, with his belief in the quasi-sacral powers of Gothic architecture, temporary expedients, like non-Gothic styles, smacked of 'Methodism'. Thus the Oratorian decision to begin with temporary churches contained an important element of policy-making. Both the Birmingham and London Oratories began with city-centre churches in converted buildings, and were followed by the purchase of suburban sites on which permanent houses, but temporary churches, were erected, following Newman's observation that collecting for a later church would be easier than for a present residence.[62]

Although they avoided expensive churches, the Oratorians undertook heavy expenditure in buying and building, even in Brompton. Yet compared with the problems which faced contemporary secular missions in London, the Oratory had considerable advantages. Its social composition, made up of converts with backgrounds of country houses and Oxford Common Rooms, was remarkable. From such convert families came not only priests but generous financial support. An example was Mrs Elizabeth Bowden (1805-1896), the convert widow of J. W. Bowden, Newman's great friend of his earliest Oxford days, who provided the St Wilfrid chapel in the present church, as well as two sons and one nephew who became Oratorians. The Oratory also drew on the support of the wider rich Catholic laity, most significantly that of the 14th and 15th Dukes of Norfolk. Finally, the Oratory, as a congregation organised on the lines of a religious order, was able to formulate and pursue policy in a fashion that eluded the bishops and secular clergy.

The decision of the Fathers to build a new church was promptly supported by a gift of £20,000 from the Duke of Norfolk. Gribble amusingly anticipated further donations in his 1885 Christmas card. Although the competition did not specify financial limits, the Fathers

27 Herbert Gribble's Christmas card for 1885 amusingly anticipates donations and furnishings for the incomplete church. *(London Oratory album)*.

36

NEW CHURCH OF THE ORATORY'S KENSINGTON

*Opposite page:*
28 A competition design by George Nattress (from The *Builder* 4 July 1885). In this drawing Holy Trinity, Brompton, gains a spire.

29 An imaginary drawing by Gribble showing the intended inner dome and vaults built of concrete (from The *Building News* 25 June 1880).

30 The laying of the foundation stone by Bishop Bagshawe of Nottingham on 29 June 1880. The ceremony was described in the *Builder* as a 'perfect muddle'. *(London Oratory album)*.

31 The sanctuary and crossing soon after the opening in 1884. The simplicity of the interior was very striking to contemporaries; its stern lines were much compromised by later decoration an furnishings. *(London Oratory album)*.

32 Cardinal Newman. A photograph taken in 1885 by Louis Barraud.

obviously had some idea of these in mind, when in 1879 they made an appeal for £20,000 to bring the church to completion.[63]

The Oratory's patrons can be explained by its special position in London Catholicism. Though somewhat at variance with Faber's 'Spiritual Mechanics Institute', the brief that Newman obtained from Pius IX setting up the Oratory specified an apostolate amongst the upper classes and the educated. At Brompton, the Oratory quickly became the church of fashion, replacing the West End former embassy chapels frequented by the Catholics of Bishop Challoner's day. Although Faber was sanguine in describing Brompton to Newman as the 'Madeira of London', his decision to establish a church in Kensington was followed by that of the Carmelites in 1862, and by Manning who established his Pro-Cathedral there in 1869.[64] Although Faber's mission to the Irish and the mechanics continued, the tone of Brompton was set rather more by ladies of fashion. We can catch this tone in a letter of Faber to Lady

Arundel: 'we get some forty to fifty people to half-past-four Benediction constantly ...it forms part of their drive. Lady Fingall says yours is (the) only church where we late dining people can worship God.'[65]

The six most generous patrons of the new church are commemorated by coats of arms in the nave clerestory windows. Three of these were pious women, all of them widowed. Chronologically, the first was Mrs Bowden, who began her gifts to London Catholicism with the church of St Thomas of Canterbury, Fulham (1847-1848). Here her architect was Pugin, but with Newman's support she insisted on the demolition of Pugin's Rood Screen immediately before the opening of the church. In 1852, with the architect J. J. Scoles, she was one of the two lay recipients in trust for the Brompton site. To the new church she gave the largest side-chapel in memory of Faber.[66] Another pious widow was the Duchess of Argyll (1809-1874), a penitent of Faber's, whose lavish redecoration and enlargement of the temporary church in 1858 detracted somewhat from the earlier argument in favour of cheap temporary churches. The inlaid stalls and elaborate sanctuary floor, made up of woods from the collection of her late husband the 7th Duke, survive in the present church.[67] The third member of this group was Mrs Daglish-Bellasis, whose second husband was the brother of two Oratorians and son of Newman's friend Edward Bellasis. She and her second husband, also magnificent patrons of Westminster Cathedral, like the Duke of Norfolk, gave the outer dome in 1895, to commemorate the tercentenary of St Philip Neri's death.[68]

33 Mrs Elizabeth Bowden, widow of Newman's Oxford friend J.W. Bowden. She was the mother of Fathers John and Charles Bowden. *(London Oratory album)*.

34 Ann, Duchess of Argyll, third wife of the 7th Duke. She was a penitent of Father Faber and a generous benefactor. *(London Oratory album)*.

35 St Wilfrid's chapel, given by Mrs Bowden as a memorial to Father Faber.

After the Dukes of Norfolk, the next most important patrons of the Oratory were individual Oratorians themselves. The site and house were largely purchased by them; the decoration of the Little Oratory in 1872 by John Hungerford Pollen, and the building of the adjacent halls of St Wilfrid and St Joseph, were the gift of Fr Sebastian Bowden, later twice Superior; the decoration of the church by the Italian, Commendatore Formilli, was largely the result of a legacy left by Fr Michael McKee.[69] In addition, many furnishings commemorate individual Fathers.[70]

*The New Church and its liturgy 1884-1903*

Although Manning moved his Pro-Cathedral to Our Lady of Victories, Kensington, in 1869, until the opening of Westminster Cathedral in 1903 both he and Cardinal Vaughan used the Oratory as their chief church. Lytton Strachey pictured Manning in *Eminent Victorians* as he 'passed in triumph from High Mass at the Oratory.'[71] The themes of the various liturgies and their properly triumphalist tone are illustrative of many

V Interior of the 1854 church in about 1865, at the moment of Solemn Benediction. This view shows the church after the raising of the roof and other improvements largely paid for by the Duchess of Argyll in 1856. The clock in the picture is the same as that below the choir tribune in the present church. (*The London Oratory*).

VI Interior of the church after the 1984 restoration.

VII The sanctuary after the 1984 restoration.

VIII The Duke and Duchess of Norfolk in 1846, when they were still Earl and Countess of Arundel, with three of their daughters: Lady Victoria Alexandrina, Lady Minna Charlotte, Lady Mary Adeliza. From a watercolour by Dartiguenave. *(Arundel Castle)*.

important aims and ideals in late Victorian Catholicism in England. There were first of all Sunday High Mass and Vespers, the seasonal or feast day liturgy, the ceremonies proper to the Oratory itself: its consecration, lasting five hours, by three bishops on April 16th, 1884, and its opening on St Mark's day 1884 by Manning, with sixteen bishops, two hundred and fifty priests, and seventeen representatives of religious orders.[72] Manning's lying-in-state, witnessed by thirty-eight thousand people, and his requiem, took place here in 1892. His successor Vaughan was enthroned in the Pro-Cathedral, but he purposely chose the Oratory for two dramatic liturgies in 1893, which were designed to highlight Catholic claims. The first was the 'frankly controversial'[73] ceremony of the reception of the *pallium* in June 1893. The *pallium,* an episcopal stole that conferred archiepiscopal jurisdiction, was usually given in Rome, but Vaughan thought an investiture by an Apostolic Delegate sent to London as 'too good a trump-card against the Anglicans to throw away.'[74] The ceremony was witnessed by all the English bishops and by four hundred priests. The preacher was Abbot Gasquet of Downside, the mediaeval historian who was about to play such a controversial role in the condemnation of Anglican Orders. The church was filled with perhaps six thousand standing faithful. Equally propagandist was the solemn dedication of England and Wales to Our Lady and to St Peter on June 29, 1893, underlining both the past and

*Opposite page:*

36 Henry Fitzalan-Howard, 15th Duke of Norfolk, as a young man. *(The London Oratory).*

37 St Philip's altar, the gift of the 15th Duke of Norfolk, decorated for his Feast Day on the 26 May, *c.*1895. *(London Oratory album).*

38 The sprinkling of the catafalque. The solemn Requiem at the Oratory for the Catholic soldiers who fell in the Boer war. *(The Daily Graphic 17 January 1902).*

39 The church decorated for the tercentenary of the death of St Philip Neri in 1895. *(London Oratory album)*.

40 *Cantus Evengelii* by A. Chevallier Tayler. This painting, exhibited at the Royal Academy in 1897, was later reduced in size. It shows High Mass at the Oratory. The celebrant at the altar is Father Sebastian Bowden; the deacon singing the Gospel is Father Gerald Lowry-Corry (1871-1929). *(The London Oratory)*.

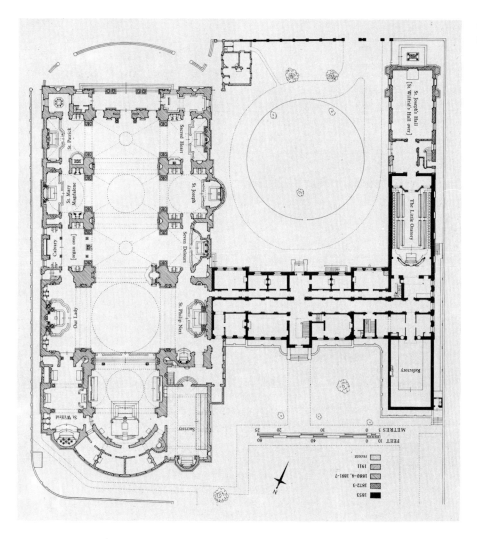

present devotion of Catholic England to Our Lady and to Rome. Though a self-conscious re-enactment of England's mediaeval title of 'Our Lady's Dowry' and of its attachment to the Holy See, the ceremony, like the investiture, was enacted in distinctly modern and Ultramontane Roman dress. Both were a prelude to Vaughan's forthright opposition to the contacts between High Church Anglicans and ill-informed Continental ecclesiastics, and to his prompting of Pope Leo XIII to scotch Anglican fantasies of Corporate Re-Union, and later, in *Apostolicae Curae* (1896), to rule on Anglican Holy Orders as in Catholic terms invalid.[75]

The Oratory also saw the official Catholic celebrations of Queen Victoria's Golden Jubilee in 1897, graced with generous recognition from the government and royal household itself, and public ceremonies on the death of the Queen, the accession of Edward VII, and for the Catholic Boer War Dead in 1900.[76] Subsequent official Catholic ceremonies moved to the new Cathedral which was opened in 1903. But the most lavish ceremonies were, appropriately, those special to the

Oratory: the celebration of the beatification of the Oratorian Blessed Juvenal Ancina in 1890; the jubilee of the London Oratory in 1899; but most of all, the tercentenary of St Philip in 1895 (plate 39). The church was decorated as for a *Quarant'Ore*, with forty-six chandeliers and over one thousand candles, for a *triduum* of Pontifical High Masses, and on the anniversary itself for Pontifical High Mass and a sermon from Cardinal Vaughan.[77] A more poignant ceremony took place late in 1894; Gribble's requiem. He died aged only forty seven, half way through the completion of his last work for the church, the façade begun to his revised design in 1891, unfinished at the time of his death but, like the dome, completed for the Tercentenary of St Philip in 1895.[78]

NOTES

1 *London Oratory Archives* (hereafter LOA), Edmund Bishop Letters, Bishop to Antrobus 18.iii.1895. For Bishop see Nigel J. Abercrombie, *The Life and Work of E. Bishop* (1959).

2 Previous guides and histories have concentrated, not on the architecture of the present church, but on other topics: Fr Sebastian Bowden's *Guide* (1893) was a polemic aimed at not entirely uninformed Protestants; *The London Oratory 1849-1949* (1949) celebrated the centenary of the community. More useful to the architectural tourist have been the many editions of Fr Kilburn's *A walk round the church of the London Oratory* (12th edition 1980), and Fr Michael Napier's *The London Oratory* (2nd edition 1983). The present author has drawn on these, and especially on the definitive history of the site, the Oratory house and churches, in *The Survey of London*, vol. XLI, *Southern Kensington: Brompton* (1983). I am grateful to Mr Peter Bezodis of the GLC Historic Buildings Division for making his text available to me before publication.

3 Gribble in *The Builder*, 15.iii.1884, pp. 386-7.

4 A. C. Benson, *The Life of Edward White Benson* (2 vols., 1899) vol. II, p. 372. Benson was warning his clergy of the lure of Rome, following the judgement against the High Church ritual practices of the Bishop of Lincoln in 1890. The Archbishop's youngest son, Robert Hugh Benson (1871-1914) became a Catholic priest and monsignor.

5 *See below*, note 51.

6 The closest parallel is Francesco Vespignani's (1842-1899) Sacra Cuore al Castro Pretorio, Rome (1879-1887); the rebuilding of the (Lutheran) Domkirche on the Lustgarten in Berlin by Julius Rachsdorf (1894); and Albert D. Guilbert's (1866-1949) N-D. de la Consolation, rue Jean Goujon, Paris (1897-1903).

7 Holy Redeemer, Clerkenwell, London (1887-1888) by J. D. Sedding; *see below*, note 51.

8 Ronald Knox, *A Spiritual Aeneid* (1918), 1950 edition, p. 62. Previously Knox had been a protagonist of the introduction of the Baroque into Anglican High Church circles, through the Society of SS Peter and Paul.

9 F. W. Faber, *Sights and Thoughts in Foreign Churches and among Foreign Peoples* (1842). Criticising the conversion of the Lowther Rooms to a church, Pugin wrote: 'Conceive the Poet Faber come down to the Lowther Rooms!!! The man who wrote of *Sights and Thoughts in Foreign Churches* hiring the Lowther Rooms.' (Pugin to the Earl of Shrewsbury, 1849, in M. Trappes-Lomax, *Pugin: a mediaeval Victorian* (1932), pp. 127-8.

10 Pugin to Shrewsbury (note 9 above).

11 *Ibid.*

12 Newman to Ambrose Philipps de Lisle, in *Newman's Letters and Diaries* (1961 ff), C. S. Dessain (Ed.), vol. XII, p. 221; Newman to Philipps, 15 June 1848, pp. 219-222.

13  Newman to Miss Giberne, 6.vi.1848 (*ibid*, vol. XII, pp. 213-215), *see below*, p. 39.

14  J. E. Bowden, *The Life and Letters of Frederick William Faber, DD* (1869), p. 370: Faber to the Rev. J. B. Morris, 21.xi.1849.

15  Pugin to Shrewsbury (note 9 above).

16  *Tablet*, 1851, p. 346.

17  J. H. Newman, *Lectures on certain difficulties felt by Anglicans in submitting to the Catholic Church* (1850).

18  *Tablet*, 1854, p. 21.

19  Manning's sermon at the opening, 25.iv.1884, in *Oratory Parish Magazine*, vol. VII, July and August 1927, pp. 119-122, 139-140.

20  Newman, *Letters and Diaries*, vol. XXX, p. 337; he also refused to lay the foundation stone in 1880 (*ibid*, vol. XXX, p. 283), justifying himself on the grounds of his split with Faber and that between the two Oratories in 1855-6 (*ibid*, pp. 329-330 and 334). His first visit to the Oratory since the 1850s took place in 1879 (*ibid*, vol. XXVII, appendix III, p. 429), and in 1880 for the celebrations for his red hat (*ibid*, vol. XXX, pp. 264, 267). But Newman did present a chalice and dispatched three Birmingham priests for the opening ceremony (*ibid*, vol. XXX, pp 340-344 and 347).

21  See pp. 41-43.

22  Nicholas, Cardinal Wiseman, in *Westminster Hymnal* (1940 edition) no. 226, p. 324.

23  F. W. Faber, *Hymns* (1862 edition) 'St Philip's House' (Burns & Oates edition, no date) no. 48, p. 278; no. 87, p. 248.

24  Faber, *Jesus and Mary* (1849), preface.

25  A. W. N. Pugin, *An Earnest Appeal on the Revival of Ancient Plain Song* (1850), p. 4 an unmistakable reference to the Oratory.

26  Bowden, *Guide* (1893), 1912 edition, p. 79; J. E. Bowden, *Life and Letters of Frederick William Faber, DD* (1869), p. 373. The confraternity was first erected in 1850.

27  S. Bowden, *Guide*, pp. 104-106.

28  *The Life and Letters of Frederick William Faber, DD* (1869), p. 391; the Irish were those of Dunne's Passage mission, Covent Garden.

29  Bowden, *Guide*, p. 102; *Tablet*, 1854, p. 209.

30  These chapels, together with those of The Seven Dolours, St Mary Magdalene, St Philip Neri, and the Calvary were also provided for in the new church (*The London Oratory 1849-1949*, p. 14).

31  J. H. Newman, *Loss and Gain, or the Story of a Convert* (1848), ed. 1904, pp. 329-333.

32  *The Catholic Weekly and Monthly Orthodox*, I, (January to June 1849), pp. 440-441; *Catholic Directory*, 1850, p. 32; Bowden, *Guide* (1912 ed.), pp. viii-ix.

33  *Rambler*, II, 1848, pp. 344-6.

34  'Oratorianism and Ecclesiology', in *Christian Remembrancer*, no. xxi (January 1851), pp. 141-165, quotation from p. 141. The author, perhaps A. J. B. Beresford Hope, also dealt with 'Popular Services' and 'Mariolatry'.

35  *Tablet*, December 1853, p. 803.

36  See p. 53 of this volume.

37  See pp. 35-36 below.

38  *OPM*, vol. VIII, April 1928, no. 88, pp. 61-62: 'it may be said that the greatest debt we owe to Father Keogh is the Church itself' (p. 61). See also Joseph Gillow, *A Literary and Biographical Dictionary of the English Catholics*, 5 vols. (London and New York, 1885-1903, vol. IV, pp. 16-17, based on *The Tablet*, 1887, p. 471. His reply to Dollinger ('Janus') was *A Few Specimens of 'Scientific History' from 'Janus'* (1870).

39  LOA, *General Congregation Minutes*, 26.vi.1878.

40  *Ibid, General Congregation Decreta* 12.xi.1878: 'to accept the offer of a marble altar from Brescia ...to be purchased by subscription undertaken by the Rev. Father (Keogh) at his own risk.'

41  For Gribble's career, see his obituary in *The Architect*, 13 December 1894, p. 378.

42  James Fergusson, *History of the Modern Styles of Architecture* (1862), p. 328.

43  For Fergusson, see Nikolaus Pevsner, *Some Architectural Writers of the Nineteenth Century* (1972), pp. 238-251; for the National Art Training School, see John Physick, *The Victoria and Albert Museum: the history of its buildings* (1982), pp. 13-15; for Moody, *ibid*, pp. 57-79, 142; and for the Ceramic Staircase, *ibid*, pp. 124-129.

**44** Fergusson, *History of Modern Styles of Architecture,* p. 81.

**45** See pp. 61-62 of the present volume.

**46** Winefride de l'Hôpital, *Westminster Cathedral and its architect* (2 vols., 1919) vol. I, pp. 21-23.

**47** *LOA: Congregation of Deputies,* 12.xi.16, 21.xii.1877; *British Architect,* 25.i.1878, p. 49

**48** *Survey of London, Vol. XLI: Southern Kensington, Brompton,* pp. 52-54.

**49** Fr R. F. Kerr in *OPM,* vol. VII, no. 2, February 1927, p. 21.

**50** *Building News* 3, 10.iii.1876, pp. 218 and 262.

**51** Adams and Kelly were architects of Our Lady, Chiswick (1885-1886), to which the High Altar from the temporary Oratory was transferred, and later of St Patrick, Soho Square, London (1891-3); G. C. Scott junior, of the altar and reredos in the Chapel of St Phlip Neri (1880-1881) at the Birmingham Oratory; Francis Tasker, of St Patrick, Wapping (1879-1880); Albert Vicars, of the Romanesque St Joseph, Highgate (1888-1889); John O'Neill with W. H. Byrne, of St Agatha, Dublin (1880-1907); and Bernard Smith of Smith, Broderick and Lowther, of the rebuilding of St Charles Borromeo, Hull in 1894-5. The only Catholic competitor whom Waterhouse ignored, George Goldie, found his scheme largely re-used for his son Edward Goldie's Holy Redeemer, Chelsea (1894).
Competitors of note in other fields of Victorian architecture who competed were H. B. Garling, E. W. Godwin, Temple Moore, J. D. Sedding (the architect in 1888 of the Holy Redeemer, Clerkenwell—see note 7 *above*) who were ignored by Waterhouse, and Edward Clarke, Gordon and Flockhart, and G. E. Grayson, who were all noticed by him.

**52** *LOA,* Alfred Waterhouse's *Report* 19 June 1878, in folders labelled 'New Church 1880-1884'.

**53** N. Pevsner, *Buildings of England: London except the cities of London and Westminster* (1952), p. 245.

**54** Fr F. R. Kerr, 'The Oratory in London', in *OPM,* vol. VII, no. 3, 3 March 1927, p. 42.

**55** George Sherrin (1843-1909), later the architect of St Mary Moorfields, Eldon St., London (1899-1902). For the role of his pupil, the future leading Edwardian Baroque architect Edwin Rickards, see ' "Architects I have known": the architectural career of A. D. Adshead', ed. Alan Powers, in *Architectural History (Journal of the Society of Architectural Historians) (GB),* vol. 24, 1981, pp. 103-123. esp., pp. 110-111 and 120. *LOA* (19.xii.1894): *General Congregation Minutes,* 4.vii.1894; Sherrin's elevation drawing, dated 1894, is at the Oratory.

**56** *LOA: General Congregation Minutes,* 26.vi.1878 and 27.vi.1878.

**57** *Ibid.,* 23.xii.1881; see also 5.i.1882 and 22.ii.1882.

**58** *Ibid.,* 25.x.1878, 7.v.1879; contract, *ibid.,* 1.vi.1881 and 28.ix.1881, at £4,500; for the dates, see Kerr, 'Oratory' *OPM,* vol. VII, no. 2, April 1927, p. 61 and no. 4, May 1927, p. 79; for Newman see note 20 *above*.

**59** *Survey of London,* vol. XLI, p. 55, *LOA*: Waterhouse's *Report.*

**60** *London and Dublin Orthodox Journal,* vol. IV, 1837, pp. 180 and 193-197; three missions had closed, but numbers remained constant at twenty-three; three new churches were built at Moorfields, St John's Wood and Bermondsey; and six between 1840 and 1850: Southwark Cathedral (1840-1848); St. John's, Islington (1841-1843); St Peter's, Woolwich (1842-1843 and later); The Immaculate Conception, Farm St., (1845-1849); St Thomas of Canterbury, Fulham (1847-1848); Star of the Sea, Greenwich (1846-1851); Our Lady of Victories, Clapham (1849-1851).

**61** *Rambler,* vol. V, 1850, pp. 11-18; the three secular mission churches rebuilt under Manning were Kensington, Chelsea and Spanish Place.

**62** Kerr, 'Oratory' *OPM,* vol. VI, no. 11, November 1926, p. 208.

**63** For Norfolk, see p. 61 of the present volume; Kerr, 'Oratory' *OPM,* vol. VII, no. 3, March 1927, p. 45.

**64** Raleigh Addington, *The Idea of the Oratory* (1961), pp. 113-114 and 122-123; Kerr, 'Oratory', *OPM,* January 1924, pp. 439-441; Newman, *Letters and Diaries,* vol. XV, pp. 166-7.

**65**   *LOA: Howard Letters,* Vol. I, p. 46, Faber to Lady Arundel, 7 June 1854, referring to the newly-opened temporary Brompton church.

**66**   Mrs Elizabeth Bowden (1805-1896), widow of J. W. Bowden (1799-1844), who was converted in 1848, was the mother of Fr John Edward Bowden (1829-1874), the biographer of Faber, and of Fr Henry Charles Bowden (1836-1906), also an Oratorian priest; Henry George Bowden (1836-1920), twice superior of the London Oratory, as Fr Sebastian Bowden, was her nephew. For Newman's comments on the Fulham church, see p. 23; for benefactions to the Oratory, see *Survey of London* (p. 55), and Kilburn, *A Walk,* p. 21; she also gave the Oratory its villa in Sydenham and possibly £10,000 for the Brompton site.

**67**   Ann, Duchess of Argyll (1809-1878), widow of John, 7th Duke of Argyll (1777-1841), became a Catholic in 1856. She was originally sent away by the Oratory verger because of her humble appearance: 'Father Faber is engaged: go off to Dr Manning, he is good enough for the likes of you.', (*Oratory 1849-1949,* p. 17); for her benefaction see *Survey of London,* vol. XLI, p. 51.

**68**   Mrs Daglish-Bellasis, married as her second husband William Daglish-Bellasis, and with him was one of the co-founders of Westminster Cathedral: de l'Hôpital, *Westminster Cathedral and its Architect,* vol. I, pp. 327-8, Kilburn, *A Walk,* p. 11. William Daglish-Bellasis' brothers, Richard Garnett Bellasis and Henry Bellasis, were priests of the Birmingham and Rome Oratories respectively. See also Kerr, 'Oratory' *OPM,* vol. VII, October 1927, p. 180.

**69**   The cost of the Brompton site was £16,000; the contract price for the house was £18,020, but £29,316 was spent; that for the temporary church was £3,500, but £5,549 was spent (*Survey of London,* vol. XLI, pp. 50-51). *The Tablet,* 1853, p. 803, attributed these expenses to the Fathers' own resources; but a lady donor, perhaps Mrs Bowden, gave £10,000, (Bowden, *Faber,* pp. 404-405; for Fr S. Bowden, see *The Oratory 1849-1949,* p. 23; *Survey of London,* vol. XLI, p. 51; for Fr McKee, *The Oratory 1849-1949,* p. 22.

**70**   The decoration of the Chapel of St Joseph in 1896 by George Aitcheson was in memory of ♭ Edmund Garnett; the marble decoration of the Blessed Sebastian Valfré altar by Thomas Garner was in memory of Fr Philip Gordon; the whole church was in a sense a memorial to Faber.

**71**   Lytton Strachey, *Eminent Victorians* (1918), 1974 edition, p. 11.

**72**   Kerr, 'Oratory', *OPM,* vol. VII, May 1927, p. 82 and June 1927, p. 99; for Manning, *ibid.,* vol. IX, February 1929, pp. 22-23.

**73**   G. Snead-Cox, *The Life of Cardinal Vaughan,* 2 vols., (1912), vol. I, pp. 12 and 15-22.

**74**   *Letters of Herbert Cardinal Vaughan to Lady Herbert of Lea,* Shane Leslie (ed.), 1942, p. 405; Kerr, 'Oratory' *OPM,* vol. IX, February 1929, pp. 23-24.

**75**   Kerr, 'Oratory' *OPM,* vol. IX, 1929, pp. 41-42; Snead-Cox, *Vaughan,* vol. II, pp. 141-230.

**76**   Kerr, 'Oratory' *OPM,* vol. IX, July 1929, pp. 121-124 and September 1929, pp. 161-163.

**77**   *Ibid.,* April 1929, pp. 61-64; May 1929, pp. 81-82; and June 1929, pp. 101-102.

**78**   Kerr, 'Oratory', *OPM,* Vol. VII, September 1927 p. 162, and October 1927 p. 179; *LOA, General Congregation Decreta,* 3.vi.1890, 10.x.1890; Gribble's obituary in *The Architect,* 13 December 1894, p. 378.

# THE DUKES OF NORFOLK AND THE LONDON ORATORY

## *John Martin Robinson*

42 Fr Richard Stanton of the London Oratory, friend and correspondent of several generations of the Howard Family. *(London Oratory album)*.

'The good Providence of God has certainly formed a link between us. He has given you and yours an opportunity of which you have fully availed yourselves of showing your devotion to His Church; and when He allows us to render you some little service, we consider it a special grace. I hope and trust that this is intended to last for generations to come.'[1] In these words in a letter to Minna, Duchess of Norfolk, in May 1864 Fr Richard Stanton (1820-1901) of the London Oratory referred to the unusually close relations which then existed between his community and the Fitzalan-Howard family. As it turned out this special link was to last for only two generations and ended soon after the death of the 15th Duke of Norfolk in 1917. For though Bernard, the late Duke of Norfolk, was educated at the Oratory School and married in the London Oratory he did not maintain the close family association with the Community there which had existed in the time of his father and grandfather. This had been not just a matter of financial patronage but close involvement in the spiritual life of the Community. Both the 14th and 15th Dukes were brothers of the Little Oratory and always came up to London from Arundel to take part in the celebration of the Feast of St Philip Neri, the 15th Duke usually acting as thurifer on these occasions. (This stood him in good stead in his role as Earl Marshal, for at the rehearsal for the Coronation of Edward VII he was able to give a ham-fisted cleric a practical demonstration of how to swing a censer properly, much to the astonishment of all those present.) Many of the priests at the London Oratory were close friends and regular correspondents of the 14th Duke, his wife and children. As well as the religious link, they shared many other interests in common including a love of architecture and books. When the Royal Society, for instance, sold part of their library (presented in the seventeenth century by the 6th Duke of Norfolk) it was a tip-off from Fr Thomas Law of the Oratory which enabled the 15th Duke in 1874 to re-acquire, through Quaritch's, a selection of volumes with special family interest including the 'Collector' Earl of Arundel's own copy of Vasari's *Lives of the Artists*, which is now safely at Arundel.[2]

The connection betweeen the Oratory Fathers and the Fitzalan-Howards originated in a chance encounter in the mid 1840s between Henry Granville, Earl of Arundel (later 14th Duke of Norfolk), and Frederick Faber (later Provost of the London Oratory) soon after the latter's conversion to Rome. The exact occasion does not seem to be recorded but a fortnight before his death the Duke commented to Faber on the chance which had brought them together while he had happened

43 Alton Towers, Staffordshire. The seat of the Earls of Shrewsbury and the likely place where Fr Faber met the future 14th Duke of Norfolk.

to be staying in a strange part of the country at a loose end. 'How good God is! You see I fell in with you, and in a part of the country where I had nothing to do.'[3] This was almost certainly at Alton Towers in Staffordshire, the seat of the Earls of Shrewsbury and the apotheosis of Catholic Romanticism with its towers and turrets, oratories and chapel by Pugin. Lord Shrewsbury was Faber's early patron at Cotton in Staffordshire. There in 1846 Faber had formed a small religious community before joining Newman's freshly established Oratory at Maryvale in 1848. The acquaintance begun through having nobody else to talk to on a wet afternoon in a large country house in the Midlands developed into a close friendship between Faber and Lord Arundel. It was cemented when Faber received Lady Arundel into the Church in January 1850, for it was she, after her husband's premature death, who transmitted a keen enthusiasm for the Oratory and its work to the next generation of the family and thus helped to win it a key place in the Catholic life of London. Fr Faber became confessor and spiritual director to the whole family, and it was largely through his influence that Henry, 15th Duke, and his younger brother Edmund (Viscount Fitzalan of Derwent, last Viceroy of Ireland) were both educated at the Oratory School at Edgbaston, and of the daughters two became nuns, Lady Etheldreda a Sister of Charity and Lady Minna a Carmelite, while Lady Margaret never married and devoted her life to working among the poor in the East End of London. As for the 14th Duke himself, Faber on his own deathbed told Newman that he had loved the Duke more than any one in the world, and during the last two months of the Duke's life from October to November 1860, Faber never left Arundel Castle but devoted himself entirely to preparing him for death.

Henry Granville, 14th Duke of Norfolk (1815-1860), was to many of his contemporaries the ideal of the Catholic layman. Burke's Peerage described him as 'amiable, excellent and highly respected' and the Comte

44 Henry Granville Fitzalan-Howard, 14th Duke of Norfolk. 'The most noble, the most humble, the most pious layman of our time.' Montalembert. *(London Oratory album)*.

45 Charles-Forbes-René, Comte de Montalembert (1810-1870). A French Liberal and strong Catholic, who had considerable influence on the 14th Duke of Norfolk's religious outlook.

de Montalembert as 'the most noble, the most humble, the most pious layman of our time'. He used his social position and his considerable wealth almost entirely for the benefit of the Church and the poor. Educated by private tutors and at Cambridge before obtaining a commission in the Life Guards, which he held for only a couple of years, the strongest influences on him were his visits to the Continent as a young man. In 1838 he was sent on a Grand Tour by his parents and while in Athens he met his future wife Augusta Mary Minna Lyons, daughter of the British Minister there. They were married in June 1839. Miss Lyons was at that time a member of the Church of England, but shared her husband's religious piety and accompanied him on his visits to France in the 1840s, where he came under the influence of the small but influential Catholic party in Louis-Philippe's Paris. They both became close friends of the Comte de Montalembert, a French Liberal aristocrat with romantic historical and religious views, which made a strong impact on Lord and Lady Arundel (as they then were). They also were impressed by the sermons of Père Lacordaire and Père de Ravignan in the church of Notre-Dame-des-Victoires, and by the revival of religion in France generally, with nuns and friars nursing, teaching, and looking after the poor; a type of religious activity extinct in England since the middle ages. It was the memory of this French experience which later made Lord and Lady Arundel the strongest and most generous supporters of Faber's schemes for 'Ragged Schools' for poor Catholics, and assorted charitable work such as food parcels for out-of-work labourers in London or cholera patients in Kent, and knitting woollen vests for orphans. A large proportion of the surviving letters from Faber to the Arundels refer to matters of this type, and Lord Arundel became Treasurer of Faber's Ragged Schools Committee.[4]

Montalembert's romantic evocation of the ancient Catholic world of Europe as it was before the Reformation in the sixteenth cetury also had

46 Arundel Castle, Sussex. The gatehouse and chapel designed for the 14th Duke of Norfolk by M.E. Hadfield were part of a scheme for reconstructing the whole castle, not completed because of the Duke's premature death.

its effect on Lord Arundel's religious outlook and, combined with a strong interest in his family's history, balanced the more practical aspects of his religious life. Thus he formed the plan of turning Arundel into a kind of Catholic Gothic utopia, where the angelus would ring again and the estate workers would have time off for choir practice. The castle would be reconstructed in a purer style, and a new private chapel be designed by M. E. Hadfield, as well as a large new parish church built for the town. His early death halted this ambitious programme and it was left to his son Henry, the 15th Duke, to carry it through to completion, to the design of different architects, from the 1870s onwards. But Lord Arundel never became an out-and-out Catholic romantic like Ambrose Phillipps de Lisle or A. W. Pugin and, partly thanks to Oratorian influence, maintained a basically common-sense approach to his Faith, as can be seen in two pamphlets which he wrote: *A Few Remarks on the Social and Political Condition of the British Catholics* (1847), and *Observations on Diplomatic Relations with Rome* (1848). The former was essentially a plea for his poorer co-religionists, the Catholic inmates of prisons, workhouses or hospitals, and the Catholic soldiers in the army, none of whom had chaplains at that time.

The influence of Montalembert and the Catholic revival in France on Lord Arundel in the early 1840s was superseded by that of the Oratory after he met Faber. From the moment that Faber left Newman in the Midlands and came to London in 1849 with a few fathers to form an independent house, Lord Arundel was closely associated with their fortunes. He tried to get the church of the Assumption in Warwick Street for them in Aril 1849. Nothing came of that and, after a spell in a former warehouse in King William Street near Trafalgar Square, Faber was able to buy Blemell House, the present site, in Brompton in autumn 1852. Brompton was an area which he described as the 'Madeira of

London' in a letter to Newman, but Newman was not particularly impressed and thought it a place of 'second-rate gentry and second rate shops', far too suburban for St Philip Neri's vision of the Oratory as an essentially urban mission. The urban spread of London westwards throughout the nineteenth century, however, long ago rectified that. Lord Arundel fulfilled Faber's expectations and, as well as chairing the committee of rich Catholic laymen which raised the money for the Brompton site, himself proved the new Oratory's principal benefactor in its early years, contributing £4,000 towards the cost of the Little Oratory chapel, the library and refectory. Faber in his correspondence usually referred to this wing of the building as 'the Arundel Wing'. Lord Arundel also paid outright for the erection of the temporary church, also designed by Scoles, with its handsome, if simple, classical interior, in 1853. It cost £5,549. In this patronage he was putting into effect the architectural views he had expressed in a letter to Ambrose Phillipps de Lisle in May 1850 when he contested Pugin's claim that Gothic was the only true Christian style of architecture: 'Why do you call one particular branch of Art, however beautiful, Christian Art? It appears to me to be at least strange in a Catholic to forget that under the much abused Churches of Roman and Greek form so many Saints have received their inspirations; and that at this moment the spread of Religion in France is conducted entirely without reference to the external form of the building!'[6]

So strong was Faber's influence on Lord Arundel that it caused a certain amount of unease in the family circle, especially among his parents. His father, the 13th Duke, was the old-fashioned sort of Cisalpine English Catholic, whose religion was a distinctly low-key affair. The diffident gentlemanly religious atmosphere at Arundel Castle was set by the ducal chaplain, Mark Aloysius Tierney, the archetype of the conservative 'recusant' priest and a close friend of John Lingard, to whose *History of England* he had contributed a foreword. English Catholics of the generation of Tierney and Lingard disapproved of things like holy water and carrying crosses in procession, and all the showier, Italianate, ultramontane character of the Catholicism associated with Wiseman and the new Catholic converts. Added to which the old Duchess of Norfolk was a Leveson-Gower, the daughter of the Duke of Sutherland, and a Protestant. These family differences came to a head over the restoration of the hierarchy in 1850. Both the old Duke and Duchess opposed this piece of 'papal aggression'. The Duchess wrote a strong letter to Queen Victoria denouncing it, while the Duke supported Lord John Russell's bill, rushed through both houses of Parliament to make the new Catholic bishoprics illegal (never put into practice, but still on the statute book) and joined the Church of England in protest. Lord Arundel on the other hand had no doubt where his loyalties lay. He supported the restoration of the hierarchy. In order not to be dependent on his father he resigned his parliamentary seat at Arundel and stood for an Irish seat in order to oppose Lord John Russell's bill in the House of Commons. His parents saw in this a direct result of Faber's influence, and developed a keen dislike for him. The Duchess thought

*Opposite page:*
47 The Little Oratory. The chapel was paid for by the 14th Duke of Norfolk. His arms impaling those of his wife can be seen painted on the ceiling.

53

48 Fr Wilfred Faber. The close friend of the 14th Duke and Duchess of Norfolk and responsible for receiving the Duchess into the Church. A daguerreotype from the 1850s. *(The London Oratory album).*

49 Minna, Duchess of Norfolk, wife of the 14th Duke. Marble effigy by Matthew Noble on her tomb in the Fitzalan Chapel at Arundel.

him an 'arrogant sacerdotal snob', though she forgave him in the end and, when her son was dying, thanked Faber for his kindness to the family and was 'almost cordial'.[7]

During this period of strongly divided opinions over the Hierarchy issue, Lord Arundel was supported by his wife, who had been gradually moving towards his religious standpoint and had become a stout friend of Faber's. The correspondence between them began in September 1849 and continued regularly till Faber's death. Lady Arundel was received into the Church by him in January 1850. To mark her conversion she offered the London Oratory a generous donation, but Faber rightly thought that large monetary contributions from distinguished postulants might be open to an uncharitable interpretation, so instead Lady Arundel gave a set of High Mass vestments. These are the splendid 'Arundel vestments', made in Rome, of cloth of silver embellished with gold needlework, and still worn every year at the Oratory on Christmas Day and on the Feast of St Philip Neri. The conversion of Lady Arundel opened the decade of closest friendship between Faber and the Fitzalan-Howards. He was particularly sympathetic to young children, and a series of charming letters survives from him to Lord Arundel's eight children. He was their spiritual director from their earliest years, and regarded Lady Minna Fitzalan-Howard's vocation as a Carmelite nun as his most satisfying achievement as a spiritual director. She made up her mind early. In December 1850 Fr Faber wrote

My Dearest Minna,
So you are seven years old, and have made up your mind to be a nun. Well now, what must you do? Must you put on a strange dress, and cut all your hair off, and go into a convent, and live a hard life? No! not just yet. Bye and bye, with Our dearest Lady's blessing it may be so. But then, as you always, always say, *but then* I cannot wait so

many, many years. Well, Sister Minna of the Infant Jesus! you need not wait. I will tell you how to be a nun at once, directly, in the Hotel Bellevue, and with the consent of Papa and Mama …To be a nun is to love Him always, and very much, and to love everybody else, papa, mamma, sisters, Boy [Henry later 15th Duke], Father Wilfrid, and all the world, because Jesus loves them so much. This is being a nun.[8]

When she was nineteen in April 1863 Lady Minna entered Rue d'Enfer, the Paris Carmel, taking the name of Sister Mary of St Joseph. She was professed on 15 December 1864 and was later for many years Novice Mistress at the London Carmel in St Charles Square. Faber's letters to her in the years 1861 to 1863, while she was preparing for this momentous step, form a substantial portion of his surviving correspondence: 'My dear Minna, keep up your spirits. You will come all right …' Many of them have been published and provide a vivid insight into Victorian Catholic piety.[9]

Perhaps more immediately attractive are the letters to Minna's younger sister Anne, nicknamed 'Sammy'. They capture most closely the image of Faber as an avuncular figure entertaining the children in the library at Arundel with his impromptu tales of 'Horumporum with the green Great-Toe' and the 'Intellectual Jackal, who was educated at the University of Good Hope'. Their correspondence begins from the moment Lady Anne learnt to write at the age of three:

My own dear little darling Sammy,
What two dear charming little notes you have sent me! I prize them so much. I only wish they could have been sealed with the end of Horumporum's thimble. And so you wish me to come back: well! it will be very soon now …Accept two enormous kisses on those great saucers of eyes, and believe me

My idolized Sammy
Your devoted slave
Ee Father[10]

After ten years of uninterrupted happiness the idyllic Catholic family life at Arundel was shattered by tragedy. The 14th Duke (Lord Arundel had succeeded his father as Duke of Norfolk in 1856) was attacked by an incurable disease of the liver. He was still only in his forties and his youngest child only a baby. When it became clear that he was not going to recover, the Duchess who had nursed him from the beginning of his illness, and was to do so till the end, turned to Fr Faber and asked him to come to Arundel to tell the Duke that there was no hope of recovery and to administer the Last Sacraments. Faber arrived on the 9th October and stayed till the Duke's death on 26th November, and for the funeral on 6th December. Canon Tierney, the ducal chaplain, was still alive but too old to cope with the tragedy, and Faber took control of everything. He wrote a day by day account to Fr Hutchison at the Oratory, and these letters still convey the atmosphere of suffocating horror and sadness in the castle at the time of the Duke's death, and by implication the importance of Faber's role in the Howard household during this period of trial:

> I was not prepared for the sight. I shd not have known him—*nor his voice*. He is a skeleton ...*I* have had to tell him. It is done—and we are beginning a General Confession ...'Well! Father—let it be a holy death, or if I am to live, let it be such a life as I have never lived before' ...The children are not to know. The duchess cannot bear it: she is with the duke all night as well as all day. She is wonderful: it is a calm, brave broken heart. Just that.[11]

And so it goes on for day after day with the Duke alternately sinking and rallying, the servants in tears, the doctor's opposition to the Last Sacraments for fear that they might kill the Duke. As the strain increased the Duchess retired to her room unable to face meals in the dining room, and it fell to Faber to keep the whole daily order going for the sake of the children, though he was not unaware of the ghastly irony of the Duke lying on water-pillows, covered with bed sores, his hands turning green, and 'we dining in grandeur' with liveried footmen and gold plate only a hundred yards away.

In the midst of 'a thousand sorrows' only the Duke himself seemed calm and peaceful. 'I never remember him so downright *happy* all eleven years' and his 'devotion to St Philip and to the Oratory seems to get hotter and hotter'.

Faber's position in the castle was far from enviable. Not only had he to look after the Duke and Duchess, deal with the doctor, Tierney and the servants but to cope tactfully with 'injudicious and meddling love', and convince the Duke to see his mother (the Dowager duchess), his sister (Lady Foley) and brother (Lord Howard of Glossop), who were all clamouring for access and blaming Faber for keeping them away. The 'opposition', especially the 'Farm Street Ladies' such as Lady Georgiana Fullerton, spread the rumour that Faber was marring 'the effect of the dear duke's glorious deathbed' and that his presence at Arundel was frowned on by everyone from 'the Queen to the servants'. But Faber paid no attention and devoted himself single-mindedly to the Duke, administering the Last Sacraments and daily confession and Communion. During the Duke's lucid moments they talked about his past life; the Duke expressed gratitude to Faber for his part in helping him to transmute his pride in 'old English feelings' into 'wider and nobler principles'. When it could not be delayed any longer, Faber told the children that their father was dying. Henry, the eldest son, was the most affected; 'He fluttered and panted like a bird one has shot and not quite killed'.

The Duke died at half-past twelve at night on 26th November, after an evening of 'quiet agony'. He tried to kiss his crucifix, whispered 'Jesus! Mary!' and placed his head on his wife's shoulder.

Faber stayed on and organised the Duke's lying-in-state in the black-draped library and the funeral at Arundel. 2,090 people filed past the coffin and all the Oratory fathers came down for the obsequies, singing the office for the dead in the library and the requiem itself in the old Catholic chapel in a corner of the ruins of the college at Arundel. The

50 The Library at Arundel Castle. Here the body of the 14th Duke lay in state before the funeral, organised by Fr Faber.

51 The quadrangle at Arundel Castle, showing its appearance at the time of the 14th Duke's death. Fr Faber disliked its gloomy north aspect and 'unutterable bastard gothic' architecture.

pall on the Duke's coffin, of black with a gold cross, was to be used again at Faber's own funeral in the Oratory three years later and again for the 15th Duke of Norfolk's funeral in 1917. When it was all over Faber's patience finally snapped. 'I *am* sick of sorrow' he exclaimed and made haste to get away from the gloomy castle, back to London. 'I am not the less disgruntled with the whole place, and tremendously impatient to breathe another air, and be in rooms the windows of which let in some light and sun, when there is sun. This gloomy north-aspected quadrangle with its quite unutterable bastard gothic takes my very wits out of me, as well as my spirits. It is a singularly odious and mournful house'.[11] In his will, the 14th Duke left £20,000 to the Oratory.

Henry, now the 15th Duke of Norfolk, was thirteen years old when his father died, and he was sent in the same year to the Oratory School at Edgbaston, Birmingham, where he was educated under Newman's own direction. His school was to have an especially strong influence on him throughout his life because he was not able to go to university (at that time there was still an embargo by the Hierarchy on Catholics attending English universities) and he was always to think of himself as a 'son of St Philip.' On his fifteenth birthday Fr Faber wrote him a letter with advice which made a profound impact, and which is worth quoting in full:

My dearest Henry,
You are a tolerably devout young gentleman: but you never had a devotion to sermons. Nearly as soon as you could speak, you desired me to preach short sermons. Now the theologians of the Church tell us that a devotion to sermons is one of the signs of predestination. So you must at least put up with the little sermon which I preach to you every year on St John's Day.

In the first place then I wish you many happy returns of the day. Yet, though I should wish you to live to be a hundred years old, and to be doing good to the Church and the poor all the time, I would most sincerely rather have you die at once than ever commit a mortal sin.

In the second place, my letter to you in 1859 was on the 'dangerous teens'. Now these teens are going on, and getting more dangerous. A boy in his fifteenth year is old enough to be a scamp.

In the third place, you are not a scamp: No, blessings on you dear little, jolly satisfactory, unbrushed, and unwashed dwarf! You are a good many thousand miles from being a scamp. But that ain't no merit to you. It is God who has done all that. So love Him more and more, and pray to Him more and more, and ask Him to give you more and more of your Papa's favourite devotion—devotion to the Sacraments.

In the fourth place, I will tell you what graces I want you to have. They are three in number.

The first is that you should be, as your Papa was, very truthful. You must hate lying, concealing, sneaking, cowardly silence, as you would hate and do hate the devil. Care for nothing and nobody, when they come across the truth. Have an immense devotion to truth. For there are few things God loves as He loves truth.

The second wish I have is that you should be very generous. Nearly all graces come out of this. Never be greedy, covetous, selfish, self-interested, or self-seeking. Here again we have to think of your Papa.

But remember, Henry, that for *you*, in your soul and with your power and means, it is easy to be generous in *great* things. But what I want is to have you generous in little things. It is *little* generosities, which bore us and come across our own wants and wishes. They are harder than great generosities and a thousand times nobler and more god-like, for what is God's daily loving providence but endless millions of tiny mercies, for the most part? Lots of men can be generous with a thousand pounds: it is only real noble men, and so real noblemen, who can be generous with a shilling! There are few things God loves more than generosity.

The third grace I want for you, and the one I want most for you, is *modesty*. This is the grandest, the holiest, the beautifullest of virtues. Be modest, in thought, in word, in look, in listening, in art, in desire. Look well to modesty, and everything else will look to itself.

Ask it of our dearest Lady daily. There are few things God loves more than modesty; for there is nothing He loves more or loves so much.

Do all this, and you'll be a 'stunning' fellow. A thousand blessings and a thousand loves from your 'ghastly father'.

F. W. Faber[12]

52 Henry, 15th Duke of Norfolk (1847-1917) as a young man. This was Newman's favourite photograph of the Duke and it still stands on the chimneypiece in his room at the Birmingham Oratory.

53 Fr Bernard Dalgairns of the London Oratory. He preached the sermon at the opening of the church of St Philip Neri at Arundel on the theme 'Jesus said to him, This day is salvation come to this house.' *(London Oratory album).*

54 The church of St Philip Neri at Arundel, built by the 15th Duke of Norfolk to celebrate his coming of age. Although designed in a French Gothic style by J.A. Hansom it is a monument to Oratorian influence.

Faber did not live to see the young Duke come of age, but he would have been gratified to know that he grew up to be the model of truthfulness, generosity and modesty.

So strong was Oratorian influence on the 15th Duke that it was rumoured in the newspapers that he was going to become a priest and join the Oratory. In fact there were no grounds for this supposition beyond the obvious devoutness of the young man. It was certainly not what Faber had in mind; he merely wished him to be a Catholic version of the Victorian ideal of the Christian gentleman. Gossip in the newspapers received a further boost when the Duke celebrated his coming of age by building a huge new Catholic church at Arundel. This was in fulfilment of his father's wish, and was very much an Oratory-inspired project. M. E. Hadfield muttered darkly that the choice of J. A. Hansom (rather than himself) as the architect was due to Oratorian influence. Though French Gothic in style, this cathedral-scale fabric was dedicated to St Philip Neri,[13] and the opening ceremony by the Bishop of Southwark in the presence of the Archbishop of Westminster was attended by all the Oratory fathers, an occasion which 'afforded a sight gratifying in no ordinary degree to the lovers of ecclesiastical splendour'. Fr Bernard Dalgairns (1818-1876) preached the sermon, in the course of which he emphasised that the building was a 'protest against the spirit of the age'. He took his text from St Luke, XIX, 9: 'Jesus said to him, This day is salvation come to this house'. The choristers of Brompton Oratory also came down specially for the occasion to sing the Mass and 'needless to say, discharged their duties most accurately and devotionally'. They sang *Ecce Sacerdos Magnus* as set to music by the Abbé Stadler, Hummel's

Mass in B flat and *Lauda Jerusalem* by Anfossi 'instrumented by a composer whose name we could not learn'.[14] The Oratorian connection was perpetuated in the altar of the south transept where a stone statue of St Philip Neri carved by Farmer & Brindley stands in a niche beneath a fretted gothic pinnacle nearly forty feet high. The Fathers' own coming of age present to the Duke was an eighteenth-century Venetian illustrated life of Saint Philip, which is still in the library at Arundel. Fr Faber had died in September 1863, but the other Oratory Fathers, especially Frs Maude, Rowe, Knox, Harrison, Keogh, Gordon, Ball, Wells, Bowden, Morris, Balston, Bagshawe, Stanton, Dalgairns, and Crewse, all kept up a regular correspondence with the new Duke, with Minna, Duchess, and her daughters for the remainder of the nineteenth century.

In many ways the high-water mark in relations between the Howards and the London Oratory came on 21 November 1877 when the 15th Duke was married there. It was the obvious choice of church. He had met his future wife, Lady Flora Abney-Hastings, on a Pilgrimage to Rome, and had become engaged to her in September at his house in the north of England, Derwent Hall, Derbyshire. The wedding was very splendid. Mass was sung by the Bishop of Southwark. The bride wore a pearl necklace which had once belonged to Mary Queen of Scots, and was attended by no less than twelve bridesmaids. The whole scene could have come straight out of Disraeli's *Lothair* (1870) and indeed Disraeli was present at the service and as a witness to the signing of the register. His own entrance to the church caused something of an impression. He described it in a letter to Lady Bradford: 'There was as great a crowd from Hyde Park Corner to Brompton as on Lord Mayor's Day. When I arrived the whole Church, very long and very full, rose, and were sadly disappointed when it was only I in a fur coat and your rustic stock.'[15]

The Duke's wedding was celebrated in Scoles's 'temporary church', but it was almost immediately decided to replace it by a grand new church on a basilical scale introducing a more authentic whiff of Rome to London. An appeal for funds was launched in May 1874, and the Duke promptly offered £20,000, making him the largest benefactor by far. As well as contributing largely to the expense of the church he also played an important role in the choice of the architect.

The appointment of Herbert Gribble has always seemed slightly mysterious; his only other significant architectural work being the Armada monument erected on the Hoe at Plymouth in 1888. The chairman of the committee for the erection of the Armada monument was the Duke of Norfolk. Gribble had worked for a time in Hansom's office as a draughtsman and had made many of the drawings for St Philip's church at Arundel, where he first came to the Duke's attention. The Duke had continued to take a friendly interest in Gribble's career, buying a watercolour of a church interior by him at an art exhibition in London,[16] and employing him to marshal the architectural evidence for the lawsuit over the Fitzalan Chapel at Arundel in 1879. This chapel was the family's burial place, and though joined on to the parish church, had become the family's private property at the time of the abolition of chantreys under Henry VIII. The vicar tried to claim the chapel as an integral part of the

55 The Altar of St Philip Neri in the London Oratory, designed by Herbert Gribble. This was a present to the church from the 15th Duke of Norfolk. He also gave £20,000 to the building fund.

parish church and employed Butterfield to prove his architectural case. There was a lawsuit and the Duke employed Gribble as his architectural witness. The Duke won, and from everything that is known about his character it is certain that he would have wished to reward him in some way. The commission for the new Oratory church was the perfect opportunity.

As well as contributing substantially to the overall costs of the church and, perhaps, having a decisive influence on the choice of architect, the Duke and his wife both contributed side altars. Flora, Duchess of Norfolk, who was suffering from an incurable illness and whose only child had, to the great sorrow of his parents, been born blind and epileptic, contributed the altar in the Chapel of the Seven Dolours. The Duke, as a splendid affirmation of his family's devotion to St Philip Neri, contributed St Philip's altar in the (liturgically) North Transept. Designed by Gribble, it is a convincing essay in sixteenth-century Roman style, with pink marble Corinthian columns, flanking figures of gilt angels, and an inset painting of St Philip Neri after Guido Reni.

The Duke continued to be associated with the Oratory after the solemn opening of the new church in April 1884. His last major contribution was to act as chairman of the committee for the erection of the memorial to Cardinal Newman facing Brompton Road. Designed by Bodley and Garner, the statue of Newman was sculpted by L. J. Chavalliaud and the carved stone tabernacle framing the statue was made by Farmer and Brindley.[17] When the Duke died in 1917 the Oratory church, to which he had contributed so handsomely, was one of the chief places where a solemn requiem was sung for his soul. His patronage is commemorated in the first stained glass window on the Gospel side of the church, which shows his coat of arms, just as his father and mother (Minna, Duchess of Norfolk) are commemorated by having their impaled arms painted on the ceiling of the Little Oratory.

56 The chapel of the Seven Dolours in the London Oratory, designed by Herbert Gribble. It was paid for by Flora, Duchess of Norfolk.

NOTES

1 London Oratory Archives. Vol. 31. Howard Letters. Fr Stanton to Duchess of Norfolk, 27 May 1864.
2 Arundel Castle Manuscripts. MD 1680. Thomas Law to Minna, Duchess of Norfolk, 9 April 1874.
3 London Oratory Archives. Vol. 29. Fr Faber to Fr Hutchison, 12 November 1860.
4 Raleigh Addington, *Faber Poet and Priest* (1974), p. 135.
5 Ibid., pp. 187, 260, 250.
6 Arundel Castle Manuscripts. Draft of letter from 14th Duke of Norfolk to Ambrose March-Phillipps (de Lisle), 11 May 1850.
7 London Oratory Archives. Vol. 29. Fr Faber to Fr Hutchison, 17 October and 24 October 1860.
8 Letters in possession of Carmelite Convent, St Charles Square, Fr Faber to Lady Minna Fitzalan-Howard, 6 December 1850.
9 Raleigh Addington, *Faber Poet and Priest* (1974), p. 322.
10 Letters in possession of Carmelite Convent, St Charles Square. Fr Faber to Lady Anne Fitzalan-Howard, 16 December 1860.
11 London Oratory Archives. Vol. 29. Fr Faber to Fr Hutchison, 9 October— 6 December 1860, daily bulletins from Arundel Castle.
12 London Oratory Archives. Vol. 32. F. W. Faber to 15th Duke of Norfolk, 26 December 1861.
13 Changed to St Philip Howard in 1973 following the canonisation of the eldest son of the 4th Duke of Norfolk by Pope Paul VI.
14 *The Tablet,* 5 July 1873.
15 G E Buckle, *Life of Benjamin Disraeli, Earl of Beaconsfield*, (1910), Vol. VI, p. 196.
16 Arundel Castle Manuscripts. MD 1679. Correspondence about Art.
17 Arundel Castle Manuscripts. 15th Duke's papers.

57 The memorial to Cardinal Newman (1896) outside the London Oratory. Designed by Bodley and Garner with a statue by L.J. Chavalliaud. The 15th Duke of Norfolk was chairman of the memorial committee.

IX The Arundel Vestments, given to the London Oratory in 1850 by Minna, Duchess of Norfolk, as a thank-offering for her reception into the Church. They were made in Rome of cloth of silver. (*The London Oratory*).

X The Dining Room at Arundel Castle. Father Faber had to keep the daily routine going while the 14th Duke was dying. He was struck by the irony of 'we dining in grandeur' with liveried footmen and gold plate, while the poor Duke was lying in agony only a hundred yards away.

# BAROQUE SCULPTURE IN A NEO-BAROQUE SETTING

## *Alastair Laing*

The Brompton Oratory possesses two of the finest ensembles of monumental Baroque sculpture in the United Kingdom. The statement will surprise many, yet it is not mere hyperbole. The Victoria & Albert Museum next door has an incomparable collection of sculpture, but despite its possession of Bernini's *Neptune* and Cornacchini's groups from Dresden, the strength of its collections does not reside in monumental works. The Oratory, by contrast, not only possesses a whole set of statues of the *Twelve Apostles* carved by the Sienese sculptor Giuseppe Mazzuoli (1644-1725), in niches in the nave and transept, but also a seventeenth century Brescian polychrome marble altar with its full complement of sculpture, in the shape of the Lady Altar. The absence of comparable works from our museums has not simply been a consequence of size—one has only to look at the rood-loft from Hertogenbosch in the Victoria & Albert Museum to see that this presented no insurmountable obstacle—it was also the result of taste. At the time when such works were being torn from their settings and put on the market, monumental Baroque sculpture had sunk to a nadir in public esteem. How then did such things come to be acquired for the Church of the Oratory? In the case of the altar, we know that it was rescued from a doomed church in Brescia in 1881, thanks to the taste and quick action of the Superior of the Oratory, Fr Keogh.[1] With the Mazzuoli *Apostles* the course of events is less straightforward, for although they originally came from the interior of Siena Cathedral, they were bought by the Oratory not from there but, on the strength of photographs, from a warehouse in Genoa in 1895.[2] Not the least piquant aspect of the whole transaction is that the *Apostles* had been removed from Siena Cathedral in 1890 after almost forty years' acrimonious debate[3], in order to 're-Gothicise' it, only to find their place, five years later, in an architectural context that employed Roman Baroque, rather than Gothic, to speak for the recovered faith of England.[4]

Yet there is a greater irony still in the ejection of the Mazzuoli *Apostles* from Siena Cathedral, for they themselves had once been *moderne* substitutes for a set of Gothic Apostles, regarded as *d'antica rozzezza*, which they had displaced as they were carved, between 1679 and 1695.[5] These earlier *Apostles* were by the sculptor-architect of the façade of the Gothic Cathedral, Giovanni Pisano, and his successors. Rather than being cast out altogether for the Mazzuolis, they were at first placed in store, from which they were brought out in 1695 to stand at intervals on the eaves of the roofs on the south side of the cathedral. Rescued from here in turn, they are now in a museum in the crypt.

58 E.E. Viollet-le-Duc, *View through the crossing of Siena Cathedral to the choir* (1856), showing Mazzuoli's *Christ* and *St Peter* in their original locations. *(Paris, Ecole National Supérieure des Beaux-Arts)*.

The urge to remove Mazzuoli's *Apostles* from the Cathedral was originally prompted by neo-classically inspired criticisms of their style. Their first serious critic, the local art historian Ettore Romagnoli (1772-1838), found fault with each statue individually, mostly for want of truth or nobility, and for defects in the drapery—which in the case of the St James he specifically lambasted as *Berninesco*.[6] Only later did the arguments come to turn on their inappropriateness and incumbrance to the Gothic cathedral. Here, the most savage polemics were those of Luigi Mussini, who claimed that inside it was: 'almost as if the two confronted rows were only waiting for the music to strike up to start interweaving in a *contre-danse*'; whilst if they were substituted for their predecessors on the roof, they would look like 'so many ungainly white birds about to take flight'.[7] They were *'una vera e propria bestemmia artistica'*, interrupting the clean lines of the nave. This last criticism suggests that part of the problem was that by the nineteenth century many Sienese were ill at ease with a convention which is perhaps more familiar north of the Alps: that of placing a set of Apostles against the pillars of the nave (although they were content to leave the bronze angel-candelabra by Cozzarelli and Beccafumi in similar positions in the choir). Certainly, they made no attempt to bring down the original Gothic *Apostles* from the roof to replace Mazzuoli's, but contented themselves with merely substituting crosses, so that the original iron attachments can still be seen.

These crosses appropriately revert to the source of Apostle-figures themselves: the liturgical stipulation that the walls of a consecrated church be adorned with twelve locations for candles marked with a cross, symbolic of the Apostles.[8] To give particularity to the symbolism in Germany, where there is even a special word for them—*Apostelleuchter* or 'Apostle-lights'—each cross may be adorned with the attributes of an individual Apostle, or with portrayals of him, whether bust-length in the form of paintings or reliefs, or fully in the round, as statues in niches or on consoles. Such statues were in some sense the result of a migration of the locus of sculpture from the exterior to the interior of churches in the later Middle Ages[9] (in the case of Siena Cathedral, it is even possible that the Gothic *Apostles* were originally intended for the façade)[10], but seem always to have been rarer in Italy. Mazzuoli's *Apostles* appear, however, to have initiated a revival of the idea in Italy in the Baroque, beginning with the famous set of *Apostles* in the Lateran Basilica, to which Mazzuoli himself contributed a *St Philip* (f. 1715),[11] and culminating in transmuted form in the set of *Founders of the Religious Orders* (1701 ff.) in St Peter's.[12]

Little is known about how Mazzuoli won the commission to replace the Gothic *Apostles*. The decision was taken in 1679,[13] and the task will have been awarded to Mazzuoli as a local son, who had not only already proved himself by executing a *Dead Christ* (1670) as an antependium for S. M. della Scala, and an *Immaculata* (1677-8) for S. Martino, but who as a result of the former had also become the protégé of Cardinal Flavio Chigi, the *cardinale-nipote* who was himself from the Sienese patriciate.[14]

Although born in Volterra, Giuseppe Mazzuoli (1644-1725) was taken to Siena at a early age, together with his four elder brothers, by their father Dionigi, a mason from Cortona. He first learnt to sculpt from his brother Gianantonio, but subsequently studied in Rome under Ercole Ferrata and Melchiorre Cafà. He was summoned back to Siena by his brothers to execute the antependium for the altar that they had undertaken in S. Maria della Scala (1670-71), but returned to Rome to execute the *Charity* (1673-5) on Bernini's tomb of the Chigi pope Alexander VII. He spent the rest of his career in Rome, becoming the principal sculptor to maintain the Berninesque tradition there well into the eighteenth century, which was further carried on by numerous nephews in Siena after his death. His output ranged from secular works such as the *Adonis gored to death by the boar* (f. 1709) in the Hermitage, and well-characterised portrait busts, to devotional sculpture and tombs —most notably those of the Rospigliosi and Pallavicini in S. Francesco a Ripa in Rome (1713-14). The *Apostles* for Siena Cathedral (1679-95) probaby rank as the single most important commission of his career.

In preparation for the task Mazzuoli made a set of terracotta models, of which that for *St Simon Zelotes* is in the Birmingham City Art Gallery, and that for *St Matthew,* together with a rejected model for another *Apostle,* is in the Ashmolean Museum in Oxford.[15] There are reputed to be further models in the Chigi-Saracini collection in Siena, which may not all be autograph—since the example illustrated in Fiorella Pansecchi's article, which is initialled *'DB',* is simply a repetition of the rejected model for an *Apostle* now in the Ashmolean.[16]

According to Pascoli, Mazzuoli executed the Apostles by dividing his time between Siena and Rome, spending the summer in the first (no doubt to the benefit of his health) and winter in the second.[17] By the time that he had completed the commission, he had so much work in Rome that he was forced to forsake Siena altogether.[18] Some fifteen years later, however, around 1710, he attempted to retire there. It was then that he executed two culminating statues that were placed under the

59 *Christ* and the *Virgin Mary,* an old dealer's photograph of the two statues that were offered, but did not come, to the Oratory. *(London Oratory album).*

60 *St Simon Zelotes*, terracotta model by Giuseppe Mazzuoli for the statue from Siena Cathedral now in the Oratory. *(City of Birmingham Museum & Art Gallery)*.

61 *St Matthew*, terracotta model by Giuseppe Mazzuoli for the statue from Siena Cathedral now in the Oratory. *(Ashmolean Museum, Oxford)*.

62 *Christ*, gilded terracotta model by Giuseppe Mazzuoli for the statue formerly in Siena Cathedral. *(Royal Scottish Museum, Edinburgh)*.

63 *The Virgin Mary*, gilded terracotta model by Giuseppe Mazzuoli for the statue formerly in Siena Cathedral. *(Royal Scottish Museum, Edinburgh)*.

crossing-dome, a *Christ* and a *Virgin Mary*.[19] Unfortunately, for some unknown reason these statues did not come to the Oratory, although we know from a photograph in the Oratory's scrap-album that they must have been offered with the rest. Perhaps there would have seemed something inappropriate in consigning Christ and the Virgin merely to places in a sequence of Apostles. Whatever the reason, the statues never even came to England, and have vanished from sight since: no doubt they went to some religious house in Italy that has kept them within its *clausura*.

Nevertheless, we are far from bereft of knowledge of what they looked like. For not only is there a watercolour by Viollet-le-Duc of the interior of Siena Cathedral, looking from the north aisle across the octagonal crossing into the choir, that shows the *Christ* against the north-east pillar looking westward;[20] but the two models for *Christ* and the *Virgin* recently appeared on the art market, were recognised by the

64 *St Peter,* marble statue by Giuseppe Mazzuoli.

65 *St Paul,* marble statue by Giuseppe Mazzuoli.

present writer thanks to a copy of the photograph in the Oratory's album in the Witt Library, and have since been acquired by the Royal Scottish Museum.[21] The *Christ* holding his Cross looks curiously like the *St Philip*, save that he, like the *Virgin*, has such multiply folded and fluid drapery, and a face so small in relation to his body, that he (and she) evidently belong to a different stylistic phase of Mazzuoli's career: so much so indeed, that the models were thought to be Genoese rather than Roman on their first appearance. It has been remarked of Mazzuoli that his style deteriorated in his later years, as he grew remoter from his original Berninian sources of inspiration, and certainly this *Christ* and *Virgin* have a mannerism of pose and wilful elaboration of drapery that may even have been factors in their rejection by the Oratory. In the *Apostles*, by contrast, whilst not always successful in giving individual physiognomies to each one of them, Mazzuoli created drapery imbued with both variety and vigour.

66 *St Matthew*, marble statue by Giuseppe Mazzuoli.

67 *St John the Evangelist*, marble statue by Giuseppe Mazzuoli.

68 *St Andrew*, marble statue by Giuseppe Mazzuoli.

69 *St Bartholomew*, marble statue by Giuseppe Mazzuoli.

70 *St James the Greater*, marble statue by Giuseppe Mazzuoli.

71 *St James the Less*, marble statue by Giuseppe Mazzuoli.

72 *St Jude,* marble statue by Giuseppe Mazzuoli.

73 *St Philip,* marble statue by Giuseppe Mazzuoli.

74 *St Simon,* marble statue by Giuseppe Mazzuoli.

75 *St Thomas,* marble statue by Giuseppe Mazzuoli.

The second major ensemble of Baroque sculpture in the Oratory, the Lady Altar, is the work of many hands. As an inscription on the altar itself records, it was put up in 1693 on behalf of the Confraternity of the Rosary by a little-known Florentine 'architect', Francesco Corbarelli,[22] along with his sons Domenico and Antonio. In its structure, it is relatively conventional for the period. It is crowned by a broken and cutback segmental pediment, with a remaining central fragment resting on a console and supporting a vase of flowers, and it has a superstructure with scrolled ends of pediment flanking a giant cartouche; but it is conceived in a series of planes, with none of the dynamic curvilinearity of Padre Pozzo's altar-designs, some of which were published in the first volume of his *Perspectiva Pictorum* in the very same year.[23] Its real distinction lies in its patterned inlays of coloured marble, whose quality suggests that, prior to leaving Florence, Corbarelli had been working for the *Opificio delle pietre dure*. The Grand-Ducal workshop specialised in work of this kind (known as *commesso di pietre dure* = 'joining together of hard stones'), partly in the form of separate panels, that could be made up into table-tops or cabinets for grand tourists and the like, and partly for its showpiece, the Cappella de' Principi attached to S. Lorenzo.

This altar was originally the centrepiece of the Chapel of the Blessed Virgin of the Rosary in the Church of S. Domenico in Brescia; hence the —for an Oratorian Church—somewhat surprising collection of Dominican saints adorning it. Devotion to the Madonna of the Rosary was originally particularly associated with the Dominicans, since the devising of the meditation on the Fifteen Mysteries with the aid of a string of beads was ascribed to St Dominic himself. It received powerful reinforcement from the fact that the Dominican St Pius V had a premonition of the Victory of Lepanto on 7th October 1571, whilst meditating upon the Mysteries, and two years later declared that day as the Feast of the Rosary.

There was already a Chapel of the Blessed Virgin of the Rosary in S. Domenico in the early seventeenth century,[25] and two features of this were taken over in the new chapel: the altarpiece of the *Madonna* by the local painter, Antonio Gandino (d. 1630), and two enormous canvases, one showing *The Pope and Emperor giving thanks for the Battle of Lepanto*, and the other the *Liberation of Souls from Purgatory*, both by Gandino's teacher, the Venetian Palma Giovane (1544-1628). The *Madonna* was installed in the new altar, but apparently as a removable screen, in front of a carved wooden statue of the *Madonna* by the Brescian sculptor Santo Calegari the Elder (1662-1719), who also carved putti-angels on the pedestal; whilst another Brescian, Francesco Paglia (1635-1714), painted further putti-angels around the image.[26] None of this came with the altar to the Oratory, no doubt because the Dominicans of Brescia had taken these images of the Virgin with them to their new home. The statue that is now in the Lady Altar is of 'Our Lady of Victories', and comes from the earlier Oratory in King William Steet. This is no longer a specifically Dominican image, but it is not inappropriate to the altar, since although the wider connotation of the image is that of the Virgin Immaculate victorious over Sin, its references to actual interventions include that of the Victory of Lepanto.[27]

No documents appear to have been published about the redecoration of the Chapel of the Rosary in S. Domenico, which included the installation of the much more lavish altar that has since come to the Oratory. The inscription and signatures on the altar itself provide the essential facts. The construction and marble inlay of the altar were, as we have seen, by the Corbarelli. Their work had also included the revetment of the walls of the chapel with marble, and this too came to England. It was used, however, not to adorn the transept arm of the church, but instead to line the hall, staircase, and dining-room of a building called Surrey House in Hyde Park Place, which has since been swept away.[28]

The sculpture of the altar was distributed between various hands.[29] The lion's share—the statues of *St Dominic* and *St Catherine of Siena* (both now in niches flanking the altar), the standing figures of *Faith* and *Charity*, the reclining *Prophets* on the broken pediment, the two adolescent *Angels* clasping roses on the arch round the niche, and the *Putti-Angels* playfully crowning the altar—is reputedly all the work of the *tedesco*, Tommaso Ruez. Ruez should also have carved one of the two angels that were formerly on corbels adjacent to the balustrade, but which are now separated from the altar and placed upon the parapet of

76 *St Dominic,* marble statue flanking the Lady Altar, by Tommaso Ruez.

77 *St Catherine of Siena,* marble statue flanking the Lady Altar, by Tommaso Ruez.

the organ gallery. These two angels display greater affinity with one another, especially in the vigour of their drapery and the ruffled, feathery texture of their wings, than they do with either of those still on the altar; but, if one assumes a greater degree of workshop participation in these more secondary figures, then there is a case for saying that the angel with outstretched arms and bare legs is indeed by Ruez, whilst the angel with clasped hands and buskins is signed by Santo Calegari (who, as we have seen, was also responsible for the original *Madonna*), as recorded by the sources. The remaining two statues—those of *St Pius V* and *St Rose of Lima*—are by Orazio Marinali, and are both signed with the initials *O. O. M.*

Not one of the names of these sculptors is known to anyone beyond specialists in Italian Baroque sculpture: who were they, and how did they come together in this commission? Brescia barely had a sculptural tradition of its own, so that it was largely dependent upon itinerant sculptors passing through the city or settling there, or on sculptors

78 *St Rose of Lima,* marble statue on the Lady Altar, by Orazio Marinali.

79 *St Pius V,* marble statue on the Lady Altar, by Orazio Marinali.

attracted by a specific commission from Venice itself. All these kinds of sculptor worked on this altar. The man who executed the bulk of the statuary, Tommaso Ruez or Ruer, is also the least known. He belongs to that interesting group of Northerners working in Venice in the latter part of the seventeenth century, who gave a new direction to its sculpture, just as their fellows did to its painting. Chief amongst them was the Fleming, Justus Le Court (1627-78), whose collaborator Ruez may have been, and whose manner he perpetuated and diffused. This manner is notable above all for its busy, restless treatment of the surface of marble, both in the drapery and in the flesh. This is indeed visible in all the sculpture ascribed to him on the Lady Altar, with the exception of the figure of *Faith*, which I should for that reason be inclined to attribute to another hand.

According to Temanza, Ruez was from that great region of wood-carvers, the Tyrol; and indeed, on his first arrival as an impoverished boy in Venice, he was apprenticed by a compatriot, a tailor called Johann Kostner, to a woodcarver, and only later learnt to work stone.[30] He sculpted statues for some of the most conspicuous new locations in Venice, including the four *Evangelists* for the façade of the Salute, *St Mark* and *St Francis* for the façade of the Redentore, the two altar-figures of *SS. Peter* and *Paul* for the high altar of St Pantalon (1668-71), and pairs of *Angels* for the *Altar of the Assumption* in the Salute, and for the church of the Ospedaletto.[31] His lost *Christ on the Cross* for the

80 *Faith* and a *Prophet (Elijah?)*, marble figures on the Lady Altar, by Tommaso Ruez.

81 *Charity* and a *Prophet (Jeremiah?)*, marble figures on the Lady Altar, by Tommaso Ruez.

82 *Angel,* marble figure on the Lady Altar, by Tommaso Ruez.

83 *Angel,* marble figure on the Lady Altar, by Tommaso Ruez.

demolished Chiesa delle Vergini in Castello was so impressive that the nuns, wanting to pass it off as a Bernini, asked him not to sign it; Ruez outwitted them by inscribing *TR* on the sole of one of Christ's feet. He died around 1696, his age unknown.

It seems undeniable that, when working in Venice itself earlier in his career, Ruez strove to create more of an impression than with the sculpture for Brescia. Even so, his Le Court-like handling of drapery is still manifest, and there are evident affinities between the heads of his *Prophets* and that of the *St Paul* in S. Pantalon, and between the head of the *St. Dominic* with that of the *St Peter* there.[32] Comparison of the standing *Angels* with those in the Ospedaletto would also support the attribution of the one with arms outstretched to Ruez.[33]

With Orazio Marinali (1643-1720), we are on better-documented ground.[34] The eldest and dominant figure of three brother-sculptors, he was enormously active and prolific throughout the Veneto. Born in Angarano, he subsequently moved with his family, first to the nearest substantial town, Bassano, and then to Vicenza, which thenceforth became his base. Although he is supposed to have learnt his art in Venice, and carved his first known commission there, the *Meeting of Christ and St Veronica* (1675) for the since-demolished Chiesa delle Vergini in Castello (once in the Staatliche Museen in Berlin), little of his work was executed for the capital of the Veneto itself—no doubt in part because of guild jealousies. Nonetheless, he is credited with assimilating and adapting the lessons of the previous generation of Northern sculptors in Venice in such a way as to form the character of Venetian sculpture in the eighteenth century. His output was of the most various: garden sculpture, altar-figures, and portrait and fantasy busts; in marble, stone and stucco.

The *St Pius V* and *St Rose of Lima* were executed during a brief sojourn that Marinali made in Brescia between 1690 and 1693. His religious sculpture, though extensive, is overshadowed by his secular work and consequently little-illustrated; however, the *St Pius V* visibly embodies the same sober, unemphatic approach as his son's *St Augustine* in S. Niccolò al Lido in Venice, whose strongly-characterised physiognomy is also strikingly similar, but for the beard.[35] The heads of Marinali's sculptures are indeed their most striking feature, and it is worth observing that the most memorable product of his sojourn in Brescia was the *Bust of Cardinal Querini*, and the set of seven fantasy busts known as *'Bravi'*, all now in the Galleria Querini Stampalia in Venice.[36]

The last sculptor to have contributed to the figures on the Altar of the Rosary is Santo Calegari, or Callegari, the Elder (1662-1717). It is fortunate that his importance for the present altar is marginal—for he only carved the vanished wooden *Madonna* and one of the two standing *Angels* now removed from the altar to the organ-loft of the Oratory—as his career is somewhat contentious.[37] He was the founder of a family of sculptors operating in Brescia from the end of the seventeenth to the beginning of the nineteenth century. The eighteenth century sculptor-cum-historiographer G. B. Carboni described him as the pupil of a disciple of Algardi's—who, Giovanni Vezzoli suggests, may have been Ercole Ferrata or Antonio Raggi, whereas Camillo Boselli more plausibly proposes Leonardo Retti, who is known to have had links with Brescia.[38] Carboni further praises him as an *homo serio*, who understood the vital importance of *disegno*, the pre-existent idea set down in a drawing. His sculpture is within the Roman Baroque idiom, without any very pronounced individuality of its own. One can say little beyond this about

84 *Angel,* marble figure formerly on the Lady Altar and now on the parapet of the organ gallery, by Santo Calegari.

85 *Angel,* marble figure formerly on the Lady Altar, and now on the parapet of the organ gallery, by Tommaso Ruez.

the standing *Angel*, which must be amongst his earliest works, shortly after the *St Roch* and *St Sebastian* in the parish church of Trescore Balneario, of *c.*1690. Why he should only have been employed to carve this one *Angel* (and the *Madonna*) is not clear, particularly since it forms a somewhat uneasy pendant to Ruez's; it seems most probable that the latter left without completing his task, which would account for the figure of *Faith* seemingly also not being from his hands, any more than the *Putti-Angels* crowning the altar.

The Altar of the Rosary stood for barely a century before the Dominican friary was suppressed in the Revolution (1797), and the conventual buildings were turned over to other purposes, ultimately becoming a hospital in 1845.[39] The church of S. Domenico at first remained in use, but the hospital soon began to expand and to require more space, and the church was sacrificed to it in 1865.[40] Romanino's superb high altar-piece of *The Coronation of the Virgin* was then sold (and is now in the Pinacoteca Tosio-Martinengo), but it was apparently not until 1885 that the church was completely razed. So it was that the then Superior of the Brompton Oratory, Fr Keogh, may have been able to see the deconsecrated altar still forlornly standing in the church when he stayed at the Brescian Oratory during his summer holiday in the summer of 1879, for we learn from extracts from his diaries, that on 31st October of that year he: 'Began subscription for the Brescia altar', whilst on 12th November: 'Gen. Cong. agreed to my undertaking Brescia altar, but 2 votes against!!'[41] This first-hand contact makes the tradition in Brescia that the altar had been sold to an English antique-dealer for 3,000 *lire* as improbable as that which maintained that it had ended up in St Paul's! The dismantled altar arrived in several loads between 22nd February and 9th May 1881, it was put up in 1883, and on 26th April 1884 Fr Keogh had the satisfaction of saying the first Mass at it,[43] the morning after the festive opening of the church itself.

NOTES

1 This is asserted by old guide-books to the Oratory. Although Fr Keogh's diaries can, sadly, no longer be found, the extracts from them in the MS volume of *Various memoranda relating to London Oratorian history* in the Oratory Library reveal that he visited Brescia on his holiday in the summer of 1879, and that the General Congregation 'agreed to my undertaking [the] Brescia altar, but 2 votes against!!' on 12th November of the same year (cf. the MS *Decreta Cong. Orat. Londin.*, vol. I, under this date, recording that it was 'to be purchased by subscription undertaken by the Rev. Father at his own risk.').

2 *Decreta Cong. Orat. Londin.*, vol. I, under 5 June 1895: 'it was resolved by a majority of 6 to 5 to accept an offer of 12 Statues of Apostles.' According to Fr Ralph Kerr's history of the Oratory, published in instalments in the *Oratory Parish Magazine*, it was the former Prefect of Edifices, Fr Charles Bowden, who discovered the statues and negotiated their purchase (*loc. cit.*, February 1931).

3 Donatella Innocenti Romano, 'Le statue degli Apostoli del Duomo di Siena ovvero una brutta pagina di storia senese', *Paragone* XXVI/309, Nov. 1975, pp. 85-100.

4 Cf. Roderick O'Donnell's article, *supra*, pp. 21-44.

5 Enzo Carli, 'Le statue degli Apostoli per il Duomo di Siena', *antichità viva* VII/6 (1968), pp. 3-20.

XI The Lady Altar, originally erected by the Confraternity of the Rosary in S. Domenico in Brescia in 1693, re-erected in the Oratory in 1883.

XII Detail of the marble intarsia of the Lady Altar, executed by Francesco Corbarelli and his sons Domenico and Antonio.

**6** Romano, *art. cit.,* pp. 87 and 97, n. 13. Criticism had been voiced earlier, by Guglielmo della Valle in his *Lettere Sanesi sopra le Belle Arti,* vol. III, Rome, 1786, p. 446, but chiefly on the grounds that the imitation of Bernini was not wholly successful, save in the drapery. He had praise for the figures of *St Andrew, St James,* and *St Peter,* but found that the rest *'hanno del tozzo'* (partake of the squat).

**7** Romano, *art. cit.,* p. 88.

**8** Otto Schmitt, *Reallexikon zur deutschen Kunstgeschichte,* vol.I, Stuttgart, 1937, cols. 830-32, s. vv. *Apostelkreuz, Apostelleuchter.*

**9** *Ibid.,* and col. 821. The apostle-lights of the Sainte-Chapelle in Paris, which was consecrated in 1248, appear to have been the first to have been held by life-size statues of the Apostles, placed against the pillars supporting the vault, thus introducing a further strand of symbolism about the Twelve: *'Sunt bases atque columnae, quibus stat ecclesia'* (cf. Francis Salet, 'Les statues d'Apôtres de la Sainte-Chapelle conservées au Musée de Cluny', *Bulletin Monumental CIX* (1951), pp. 135-56).

**10** Carli, *art. cit.,* pp. 4-5.

**11** Frederick den Broeder, 'The Lateran Apostles', *Apollo,* May 1967, pp. 360-65.

**12** Robert Enggass, *Early Eighteenth-Century Sculpture in Rome,* Pennsylvania State University Park & London, 1976, pp.44-45.

**13** Valentin Suboff, 'Giuseppe Mazzuoli', *Jahrbuch der preuszischen Kunstsammlungen* 49 (1928), p. 37, n. 4.

**14** Fiorella Pansecchi 'Contributi a Giuseppe Mazzuoli', *Commentari X/1* (1959), pp. 35 ff.

**15** Exh. cat. *Faces and Figures of the Baroque,* Heim, London, Autumn 1971, no. 64; *Exhibition of Seventeenth and Eighteenth Century Italian Sculpture,* Colnaghi's, London, (1965), nos. 19 and 20, pl. XIV, and *62nd Annual Report of the NACF,* London, 1965, p. 18, pl. II.

It is a curious (and not previously remarked) fact that, although always referred to as the Twelve Apostles, the statues in the Oratory are in fact of eleven of the original Apostles, together with St Paul but not St Matthias (the substitute for Judas). The two Evangelists, St Mark and St Luke, are sometimes included in cycles with the Apostles, so that it is possible that the second model of an Apostle in the Ashmolean (since he holds a book) was intended for one of these, without his identifying Beast, the Lion or the Ox. There are, however, only fourteen pillars forming a processional way up through the nave to the crossing in Siena Cathedral, so, once it had been decided to have the statues of Christ and the Virgin as well, there would have been no place for the two Evangelists who were not Apostles.

**16** Pansecchi, *art. cit.,* p. 38 and pl. XIX, fig. 7. Amongst those with reasons for duplicating Giuseppe Mazzuoli's models was his nephew Bartolomeo, who executed a set of full-scale replicas of the *Apostles* in stucco for the Collegiata of Sinalunga.

**17** Lione Pascoli, *Vite de' Pittori, Scultori ed Architetti Moderni,* vol. II, Rome, 1736, p. 479.

**18** *Ibid.,* p. 480.

**19** *Ibid.,* p. 482.

**20** Exh. cat. *Le voyage en Italie d'Eugène Viollet-le-Duc 1836-1837,* Ecole nationale supérieure des Beaux-Arts, Paris, 1980, no. 222. I am indebted to Fr Michael Napier for bringing this to my attention. The position of the *Apostles* and of the *Christ* and the *Virgin* are recorded by successive guide-books to Siena and its cathedral, notably: G. A. Pecci, *Ristretto delle cose più notabili della Città di Siena,* Siena, 1761, p. 10; Giovacchino Faluschi, *Breve relazioni delle cose notabile della Città di Siena,* Siena, 1784, p. 20; Ottavio Fratini and Alessandro Bruni, *Descrizione del Duomo di Siena,* Siena, 1818, p. 75. Cf. also *Correspondence between Frances, Countess of Hartford and Louisa, Countess of Pomfret,* 2nd ed., London, 1806, vol. I, p. 143.

**21** Exh. cat. *Seven Centuries of European Sculpture,* Heim Gallery, London, 1982, nos. 21 & 22; *National Art Collections Fund Review 1983,* pp. 118-119, no. 2973.

**22** The inscription at the left end of the altar reads: D. O. M. VIRGINI ROSARIAE ARAM POSVIT CONFRATERNITAS ANNO MDCXCIII. That at the other end reads: D. O. M. FRAN.$^{VS}$ PATER DOM.$^{VS}$ ET ANT.$^{VS}$ EIVS FILII DE

CORBARELLIS FLORENT. ARCH. In this context, *architecti* simply means designers and constructors. Despite their stated Florentine origin, there does not appear to be any record of activity by Francesco Corbarelli and his sons in Florence —or indeed elsewhere in Brescia. They would anyway appear to have been settled from an early date in Vicenza. In 1669-70 a Francesco Corberelli [*sic*], and his sons Domenico and Antonio, were associated with Fra Giorgio Bovio of Feltre in the construction and decoration of the splendid high altar of the Dominican church of S. Corona in that city: '*ex marmoreis lapidibus eleganter intersitis juxta artificium quod vocant florentinum*', although the marble inlay is only signed by Antonio (cf. *Catalogo delle cose d'arte e di antichità d'Italia: Vicenza I: Le chiese,* ed. E. Arslan, Rome, 1956, p. 58). In 1679, a Benedetto Corbirelli [*sic*] designed the steps up to, and additional ornament of, the raised choir of Vicenza Cathedral (cf. Antonio Magrini, *Notizie Istoriche descrittive della Chiesa Cattedrale di Vicenza,* Vicenza, 1848, p. 92). The next year this Benedetto (now described as '*Veronese*') was invited by the Duke of Modena to introduce the art '*del lavorar di bassorilievo di pietre dure al modo di Firenze*' to his dominions, and brought with him his two sons and a '*segatore*'. A letter of his of 7th November 1680 describes his work—which was chiefly for items of furniture—and details his journeys to appropriate quarries for the various semi-precious stones employed (cf. Giuseppe Campori, 'Della lavorazione del porfido e delle pietre dure d'intarsio e di commesso nella corte degli Estensi, *Atti e Memorie delle RR. Deputazioni di Storia Patria per le provincie dell' Emilia,* Nuova [Seconda] Serie, vol. IV, pt. I, Modena, 1879, pp. 33-36). They are recorded as working in Modena up until 1689, and the eldest son, Antonio, by that time based in Verona but working on an altar in S. Lucia in Bologna, sought employment there again in 1701. The fact that both 'Francesco' and 'Benedetto' Corberelli had two sons, one of whom was called Antonio, makes it virtually certain that they are one and the same person, no doubt baptised as Francesco Benedetto, and alternating between the two Christian names. It is also not without significance that the Vicentine Orazio Marinali both carved the gessoed wooden *Angels bearing the Instruments of the Passion* for 'Benedetto' Corbarelli's embellishment of the choir of Vicenza Cathedral in 1679, and two of the marble *Saints* upon 'Francesco' Corbarelli's Brescian altar.

23  It should perhaps be stated here that the bronze candelabra held by putti-angels, which do not belong to the original altar, are copies of those cast by Carlo Spagna for Padre Pozzo's Altar of St Ignatius in the Gesù, which were made for the chapel of Cardinal Howard's *Palazzo* in Rome, and came to the Brompton Oratory after his death in 1892.

24  Cf. Ant. Zobi, *Notizie storiche sull'origine e progressi dei lavori di commesso in pietra dura,* Florence, 2nd ed. (1853), pp. 127 ff. Although there is no apparent mention of Corbarelli in the lists of workers in the *Opificio delle pietre dure* given there, or elsewhere in the literature, the constant allusion to his Florentine origins can only point to an at any rate unofficial apprenticeship there.

25  Bernardino Faino, *Catalogo delle Chiese di Brescia,* MS of 1630-69, ed. Camillo Boselli, *Commentari dell'Ateneo di Brescia (Supplemento),* 1961, p. 72 (MS f. 32 retro); Francesco Paglia, *Il Giardino della Pittura,* MS of c.1663-75, ed. Camillo Boselli, *Commentari dell'Ateneo di Brescia (Supplemento),* 1967, vol. I, p. 354 (MS f. 286).

26  Francesco Maccarinelli, *Le Glorie di Brescia,* MS of 1747-51, ed. Camillo Boselli, *Commentari dell'Ateneo di Brescia* (Supplemento), 1959, p. 62 and suppl. p. 2; [G. B. Carboni], *Le pitture e sculture di Brescia,* Brescia, 1760, pp. 89-90.

27  As witness the superb monstrance of 1708 by Johann Zeckl belonging to the *Kongregationssaal* of Maria de Victoria in Ingolstadt. This was originally made for the (since demolished) Oratory established by the Jesuits for the townsfolk of Ingolstadt, which gave its name to the former Oratory of the university students, to which it was subsequently transferred.

28  Fr H. S. Bowden, *Guide to the Oratory, South Kensington,* London, 1912, pp. 57-58. The house belonged to Cyril Flower, later Lord Battersea, and was latterly numbered no. 7, Marble Arch (cf. *Survey of London,* vol. XLI, *South Kensington: Brompton,* London, 1983, p. 57).

29  [G. B. Carboni], *Le pitture e sculture di Brescia,* Brescia, 1760, p. 90. Carboni was

himself a sculptor, as well as the historian of the fine arts in his native city, so that, writing about an altar put up within living memory, there is some reason to trust the unusually detailed information that he gives about its sculpture, which is further borne out by the statues that are signed. His indications are followed by subsequent guide books to Brescia.

**30** Tomaso Temanza, *Zibaldon,* MS of 1738-78, ed. by Nicola Ivanoff, Venice, 1963, pp. 89-90.

**31** Camillo Semenzato, *La Scultura Veneta del Seicento e del Settecento,* Venice, 1966, pp. 25-6 and 89-90.

**32** Temanza/Ivanoff, pls. XXI and XXII; Semenzato, pls. 29-30.

**33** Semenzato, pls. 31-32.

**34** Carmela Tua, 'Orazio Marinali e i suoi fratelli', *Rivista d'Arte* XVII (1935), pp. 281-322; Semenzato, *op. cit.,* pp. 33-37 and 96-100.

**35** Tua, *art. cit.,* fig. 8.

**36** Tua, *art. cit.,* fig. 5; Semenzato, *op. cit.,* pl. 70.

**37** The most complete account of Santo Calegari and his sons is that given by G. Vezzoli in the *Dizionario Biografico degli Italiani,* vol. XVI, Rome, 1973, *sub vocibus,* but these entries have been criticised by C. Boselli in an article in *Brixia Sacra* 10 (1975), nos. 4-5, pp. 157-61, which I have not been able to consult.

**38** G. B. Carboni, *Notizie istoriche delli pittori, scultori, ed. architetti bresciani,* MS of 1775/6, ed. C Boselli, *Commentarii dell'Ateneo di Brescia (Supplemento),* 1962, p. 23; G. Vezzoli, in *Storia di Brescia* III, Brescia, 1964, pp. 408-416, and in the entry cited in the note above; C. Boselli, 'Fatti, opere, notizie per la storia della scultura in Brescia nei sec. XVII e XVIII', *Arte Lombarda* 37 (1972), pp. 134-5.

**39** Monˢ.Luigi Francesco Fè d'Ostiani, *Storia, Tradizione, e Arte nelle vie di Brescia,* 2nd. ed., Brescia, 1927, pp. 84-9.

**40** *Storia di Brescia* IV (1964), p. 412. In Fr H. S. Bowden's more colourful version (*Guide to the Oratory,* 1912, p. 55), 'church and chapel, having been previously stripped, were levelled to make room for some public baths' in 1885.

**41** MS vol. of *Various memoranda relating to London Oratorian history,* p. 222.

**42** Tua, *art. cit.,* p. 310.

**43** *Various memoranda,* pp. 94 and 223.

86 The Library from the main
door.

# THE LIBRARY AND ITS BENEFACTORS

## *Richard Price*

To many Oratory parishioners the 'Oratory Library' is the small St Gregory's Library in the porch of the church, with its tall and handsome premises and useful collection of English Catholic classics, There is no reason why they should be aware of the incomparably richer collection, in a far more imposing setting in a distant wing of the house, that makes up the private library of the Oratory fathers. Originally, in 1854, a special stairway was constructed to enable the laity to reach the library without entering the enclosure of the fathers; but after only five years that stairwell was converted into a series of rooms with a less noble and more hygienic purpose. As the library collection began to build up, it had become clear that antique volumes of theology and church history in the tongues of Latin, Italian and French were of no direct use to the laity: the lore the library contained needed to be communicated to the faithful through the writing and preaching of the Oratory fathers. And it was this that was the purpose of its existence: in the great task the London Oratory first set itself—the task of introducing the Catholics of London to the riches of continental Catholicism after the restrictions of the Recusant period—a first-class library of Continental theology was an essential tool, to educate the fathers in the great tradition which they had a solemn responsibility to transmit, and which, as converts, they had themselves to imbibe through reading. Therefore, to study the history and character of the Oratory Library is not to explore an asylum where, over the years, fathers have escaped from pastoral responsibilities, but to examine an essential inspiration and guide for this very apostolate.

On passing through the double door into the library, a visitor is first impressed by the appearance of the main room—large, well-proportioned, with a patterned wooden floor and counters, and fine Victorian fittings. The stages of building and furnishing may be briefly given. The original west wing of the house, made up of the library above and the Little Oratory below, was built in 1854 at the expense of Henry Granville, Earl of Arundel and Surrey, later fourteenth Duke of Norfolk. The furnishing of the library followed over the next half century, each stage paid for by some individual father with a special love for the community library: in 1860 the main room of the library up to the gallery was fitted and equipped, with the parquet floor just mentioned and shelving of the best quality mahogany; in 1872 shelves were installed at the gallery level, and the small librarian's room fitted up; in 1908 the vestibule to the library was furnished, soon to contain a new card catalogue, while finally in 1910 the ceiling of the main room was decorated with rosettes in grisaille. Since that date the appearance of the library has not altered:

the light-fittings may have been rewired, but they are still Edwardian in design, while the wooden fittings remain exclusively Victorian; and, as we shall see, the books themselves, despite more recent additions, remain predominantly a nineteenth-century collection. What for its founders was a primarily practical design in a contemporary style has already become a period piece, with a feeling of suspended time, of a refinement not of our age.

But before we begin to sample books from the shelves and examine the history of the collection, let us withdraw into the librarian's room, the inner sanctuary whose huge desk, dark paper ceiling and elaborate fireplace with a bust of St Philip create an atmosphere in particularly strong contrast to that of modern London. On the shelves we find a collection of 3,000 nineteenth century Catholic pamphlets, well bound

87 The Library from the far end. The left-hand gallery door leads to the librarian's room.

and indexed, still of importance for students of church history. In the cupboards beneath and around recline—some more, some less sorted and arranged—manuscripts of Oratory fathers, forming a main part of what may with convenience, though with slight pomposity, be called the London Oratory Archives.

Pride of place in the Oratory Archives must go to the most important collection outside the Birmingham Oratory of letters by Cardinal Newman, and the only collection of note of letters by Father Faber. The Newman collection amounts to 1,100 letters, consisting of a major series of letters to Faber (starting in 1838, at the height of the Oxford movement), letters to other London fathers (extending down to 1887) and numerous letters to members of the Bowden family (a family that provided the London house with both priests and benefactors). In addition to the letters there are a few unimportant notes in Newman's hand, including some unpublished verse in Latin and English. The correspondence between Newman and the London Oratory is notoriously painful, because of the breach between them in 1855, that resulted from disagreement over the hearing of nuns' confessions; the pros and cons of the case are set out fully in a number of dossiers, some by Birmingham and some by London fathers, also kept in the archives. Relations between the two houses subsequently improved, as is instanced by Newman's stay in the London house for a week in 1881. In the context of the present centenary a melancholy interest attaches to a dossier of letters of 1884 between the London and Birmingham fathers and the Duke of Norfolk over an invitation to Cardinal Newman to attend the opening of the new church; Newman's decision not to attend, apparently out of fear that his presence might create a false impression of interdependence between the two houses, emerges strongly as due to excessive delicacy rather than any desire to reopen the wounds of thirty years back.

The Newman letters in the London Oratory Archives are balanced by the collection of letters written by Father Faber. This collection of Faber's correspondence is admittedly not comparable to that of Newman's correspondence at Birmingham, since it is far from complete: since Faber did not keep copies of the letters he sent, the collection consists only of letters received back after his death, mainly in preparation for the *Life and Letters of Frederick William Faber* compiled by Father John Edward Bowden (1829-1874) in 1869. This volume printed a judicious and lively selection, which has been supplemented recently, in 1974, by a new selection, published as *Faber Poet and Priest*, by Father Raleigh Addington (1926-1980), also of the London Oratory; there remain a large number of spirited and revealing leters that still await publication. Faber emerges from these letters as a singularly direct and characterful correspondent, even by the high standards of Victorian letter-writing. It is unfortunate that, apart from the letters from Newman and a few others, the other side of the correspondence is lost, since Faber did not usually preserve the letters he received.

By modern standards, Faber the writer is more appealing in his letters than in his published words on spirituality; yet the latter are ultimately

88  Undated manuscript verses by Newman. *(London Oratory Library).*

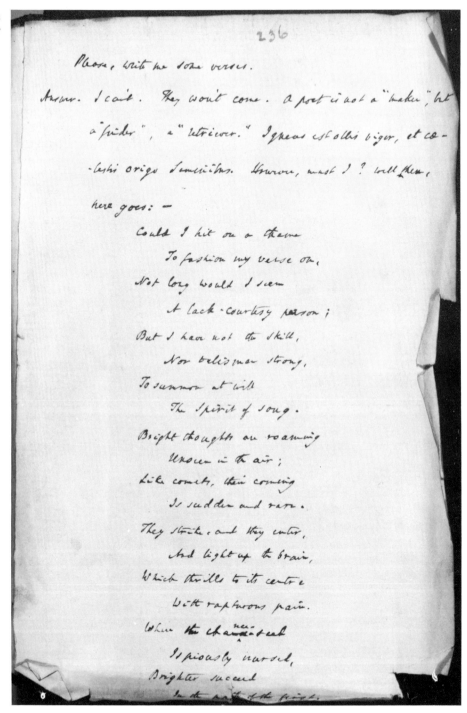

more revealing of the spirit of the Catholic revival, and here the London Archives suppplement significantly the published volumes. The neat copies of three of the eight treatises and of many of the hymns (donated to the library not by Faber himself but by later benefactors) reveal, of course, little beyond the elegance and minuteness of his handwriting; but the very numerous notes for sermons and conferences indicate well the punctilious precision of Faber's thought, before he worked up the purple passages that give the published volumes their deceptively effusive feel. These Catholic manuscripts are supplemented by manuscripts from Faber's Anglican period, which (apart from the letters) have been completely ignored by his biographers: the Oratory collection includes a revealing juvenile novel in largely epistolary form, *Letters of a young student,* written when Faber was still at Harrow, and numerous full texts of sermons, which are important for us, since Faber's Catholic sermons were never written out in full, and only summary notes survive; Newman too was of the opinion that part of becoming a Catholic was to stop preaching from a script.

If the letters of Newman and Faber are the most important sources for the early history of the London Oratory, they are supplemented by a variety of material in the archives. The house has preserved all its legal documents, including not only wills and property transactions but many ecclesiastical grants, including documents signed by Pope Pius IX and by Cardinals Antonelli, Wiseman and Manning. The grants of spiritual privileges directly by Pius IX support the story, told in Bowden's Life, of Father Faber at the end of a private audience presenting the Holy Father with a petition for a daily plenary indulgence for the Oratory church. The Pope was momentarily taken aback and referred Faber to the Congregation of Rites; 'Ah, Holy Father,' replied Faber, 'you can do it yourself, if you will.' At this the Pope chuckled, and signed the paper. But more continuous and illuminating than the legal documents are the official decrees of the Congregation, which now fill several volumes and include, because of the democratic nature of Oratorian government, many details of life and practice that in more authoritarian communities would not have been recorded. A further extensive body of material is made up of the archive's large though haphazard collection of letters, diaries and other manuscripts of many of the earlier fathers, most notably Faber's chief companions, including Fathers Hutchison, Dalgairns and Gordon. It is perhaps natural that this material is fullest for the period of the house's foundation and main development, down to about 1870, and markedly thin for the twentieth century. Yet of the fathers subsequent to Faber's first disciples there are three who are well represented in the archives—Father Philpin de Rivière, Sebastian Bowden and Ralph Kerr.

Father Félix Philpin de Rivière (1814-1907) was unusual for an Oratorian in that he had had an active career as secular priest and founder of an order of nuns in his native France before joining the London Oratory, where he died at the age of ninety-three. Although his personal saintliness earned him the position of Confessor to the Congregation for over thirty years, he never quite acclimatized himself to London. His imperfect knowledge of English protected him from the burdens of preaching and pastoral work; instead, he devoted himself to writing, partly under his own name, partly under the appropriate *nom de plume* 'L'Ermite de Brompton'. His various books and contributions to

89 Father John Bowden. *(London Oratory album).*

90 Father Faber. This anonymous portrait was perhaps painted immediately after his death. *(The London Oratory).*

French periodicals are characterful, if quaint, illustrations of the heart rather than the intellect of nineteenth century Ultramontanism: typical is a treatise entitled *La physiognomie du Christ, le plus beau des enfants des hommes.* His manuscript autobiography, preserved in the archives, is of more permanent interest, both for its reminiscences and for the touching humility it breathes: Father Philpin tells how he was taught by Father Faber to adopt as his own the Philippine motto of 'loving to be unknown' and remarks on his work as writer and spiritual director, 'La divine Providence a béni mon silence plutôt que ma parole.' Particularly indicative of the spirit of the London house is the correspondence between Faber and Philpin on his application to join the community. Faber first touched tactfully on the doubt as to whether a French priest would feel at home in an English community: 'Nous Anglais, nous sommes des rudes gens: même dans nos bontés, il n'y a pas toujours toute la délicatesse et la considération désirable.' He then proceeded to list firmly the errors of French Catholicism that Philpin had explicitly to renounce: he demanded 'horreur absolu' towards 'les libertés de l'Eglise Gallicane, le rigorisme au confessional, la réserve envers la Sainte Vierge en vue des protestants' and 'relative' disapproval of Bossuet and 'les Conciles Généraux'. Fortunately, Philpin could reassure him that Jansenism and Gallicanism were by now movements of the past.

If Father Philpin may illustrate for us the characteristic spirituality of the London Oratory, with its humility and lack of ambition, we may turn to Father Sebastian Bowden (1836-1920) for an example of the active face of its apostolate. In relation to the centenary of the church, it is worth recalling his personal involvement in the decoration of the sanctuary and construction of the porch and dome, and also his influence on the spirit of Oratorian ceremonies, which he insisted had to be conducted with the strict precision of a military parade. The archives contain many of his manuscript sermons and conferences, which bear out his reputation as a solid and effective preacher; we have also a list of his converts, who in the forty years of his active ministry numbered nine hundred and twenty-seven. Although Sebastian Bowden's contribution as a writer and translator was respectable, above all in his compilation of the *Miniature Lives of the Saints*, it is a third figure to whom we shall turn to illustrate the work of London Oratorians in research and writing. Father Ralph Kerr (1874-1932) filled the rôle of historian of the community. Our archives include his typescript work in several volumes on foreign Oratories and, above all, his own annotated copy of his *The Oratory in London,* published in monthly instalments in the Parish Magazine from 1926 to 1932; this full and lively narrative, based on archival material, the contemporary press and personal knowledge, covers principally the period from 1845 to 1890. He supplemented it with a manuscript volume of notes, which add many fascinating details for the period down to 1931, including a full and indiscreet account of the strange drama that attended the decoration of the nave of the church in around 1930, the decoration that the present cleaning has just revealed in its pristine splendour. Father Kerr's work remains the principal source for the history of the London Oratory; the biographical material in the present essay, for instance, largely derives from his work.

But let us now leave the archives and the librarian's room, and proceed into the main hall of the library. From the gallery where we stand, the main shape of the collection is already apparent: antique volumes and well-bound nineteenth century editions are equally in evidence, while more recent acquisitions are concentrated discreetly in a few sections, and do not seriously dilute the, for us antiquarian, character of the collection. It would have been possible to banish all the more recent publications out of the main library, to render the appearance of antiquity still more venerable; but who then would ever enter it? The library would become like those of the great senators of Rome, described by the historian Ammian in the fourth century AD as 'shut up for ever like tombs'. But the need to preserve the character of the main room does restrict the addition of new purchases, which have to be limited to the trickle of Catholic publications that will maintain their importance over the years.

Pride of place in our account may be accorded to the library's collection of Oratoriana, which now resides not in fact in the main hall but in the anteroom of the library, as the first and most obvious point of call. In a symbolic arrangement, shelves of literature on St Philip Neri and the Oratorian *beati* are flanked on the left by the works of Father Faber and on the right by those of Cardinal Newman. The section on St Philip contains, in addition to modern works, numerous editions of the early lives of the saint, including first editions of the lives by Gallonio

(1600) and Bacci (1622), written and published before the saint's canonization. One oddity, more to be admired than imitated, is the *Via Lactea* of 1680, a life of St Philip compiled by a priest of Valencia, in which dedication, preface and text are made up entirely, apart from proper names, of verses and phrases culled from the Vulgate—one of the most elaborate centos ever produced. Also worthy of note is the first English life of the saint, an abridged translation of Bacci printed in Paris in 1659; this Recusant publication displays a concern to adduce the miracles of St Philip as evidence in favour of ecclesiastical miracles, and buttresses the argument with an appendix on those reported from the convent of Port Royal, a linking of the Oratory and Jansenism that must have horrified Father Faber if he knew of it. To proceed to the section devoted to Faber, the huge popularity his works used to enjoy is evidenced both by virtually complete translations into Italian, French and German (including German verse translations of most of his early poetry) and also by many small volumes of elegant extracts for use during meditation. The Newman section contains as its core a complete set of his works, donated by the Cardinal himself in 1881; the generosity of the Birmingham Oratory has continued in recent years with the gift of each volume of the *Letters and Diaries*, now approaching completion. Of the Oratorian miscellanea that fill up the rest of this section of the library, a special interest attaches to a collection of original libretti of oratorios performed at the Florence Oratory in the 1690s, a reminder of the dominant contribution made by the Italian Oratories to the development of the great musical form which derives its very name from 'Oratory' as the public devotions in Oratory churches.

Let us now retrace our steps into the main hall of the library; the great bulk of the Oratory collection, totalling some 40,000 volumes, lies before us. What short tour can we devise, not to weary our visitors, not to choke their lungs with the dry dust of bibliophilic antiquarianism? Perhaps their attention will best be sustained, their interest stimulated, if we approach the contents of the library by reference to the main benefactors who over the years built up the collection; in words from the Epistle to the Hebrews now inscribed on the entrance to St Wilfrid's Chapel, 'Remember your leaders'.

Let us start with Father Faber himself. His Anglican collection of books he was obliged to dispose of, because of temporary financial embarrassment, shortly before his conversion; but this made him subsequently all the more energetic in building up a collection to deepen his new allegiance. During his stays abroad in 1846 and later he was particularly engaged in acquiring the foundation for the Oratory library, and the friends he made in bibliophile circles continued to send books to him in London; his collection amounted to some 3,000 volumes by his death, and was incorporated into the library. One might wonder how a man as active, not to say restless, as Father Faber had time for breadth or depth of reading, but time he found or rather made, as is proved by his own writings: their rather flowery style should not disguise the real erudition that lay behind each volume. In 1858, when planning a book on the life of heaven, on 'empyreology' as he called it, he had, as he

*Opposite page:*
91 Original manuscript of Faber's hymn 'Jesus, my Lord, my God, my all'. *(London Oratory Library).*

Corpus Xti.
—

1.                    "[............]"

Jesus! my Lord, my God, my All!
    How shall I love Thee as I ought,
And how revere this wondrous gift
    So far surpassing hope or thought!
            Sweet Sacrament! we Thee adore;
                O make us love Thee more and more!

                    2.
Had        But
[crossed out] St Mary's sinless heart
    To love Thee with, my dearest King!
O with what [crossed out] bursts of fervent praise
    Thy goodness, Jesus! would I sing.
            Sweet Sacrament! we Thee adore;
                O make us love Thee more and more!

                3.    "Putting into ye monstrance!"
I see! within a creature's hand
[Reposing] The vast Creator deigns to be,
[And], infantlike, [crossed out] as though
        On Joseph's arm or
    [crossed out] Mary's knee.
            Sweet Sacrament! we Thee adore;
                O make us love Thee more and more!

                    4
My Body, Soul, and Godhead, all!
    O mystery of love divine!
I cannot compass all I have
    For all Thou hast and art are mine!

wrote, 'Spain and Germany scoured for books'; and such acquisitions he certainly read. The French *Dictionnaire de Spiritualité,* in a fascicle published in 1964, commends Faber highly for his solid theological culture, for his knowledge of the byways as well as the highways of spirituality, especially of the finest writers of all, those, of course, in the French tradition.

As for the contents of Faber's collection, besides the miscellaneous volumes to be expected in the library of any educated person, we find a special emphasis on spirituality and hagiography. One particular group of acquisitions may be singled out, both as an example of his taste and for its own interest: the accidental but adequate evidence of his name in a fly-leaf reveals that he was the acquirer of a collection of sixty-four volumes from the library of the Charterhouse at Dülmen in Westphalia. The uniform bindings are eighteenth century, and the house survived till 1802, but all save ten of these volumes belonged to its library in the early seventeenth century, and so give an interesting impression of the reading of a Carthusian at that date—spiritualia rather than dogma or hagiography, with a particular taste for Jesuit writings such as the works of Alvarez de Paz, though some Carthusian classics are included, notably the first printed editions of several of the works of the great Denys the Carthusian, and such key works of Carthusian history as Dorland's *Chronicon Cartusiense.* We may note that these books are all in Latin (including Latin translations of Walter Hilton and Ruysbroeck), and that the vast majority were printd in the Rhineland itself. Of particular interest are three volumes autographed by the well-known Carthusian writer Theodore Petreius, who was Prior of Dülmen from 1612 to 1619. One of these inscriptions is characterful: 'This book was offered as a gift in 1618 to his beloved brother Dom Heinrich Moldeck, Procurator of the Charterhouse of Dülmen, by brother Theodore Petreius, once

92 The Charterhouse at Dülmen, from an old print.

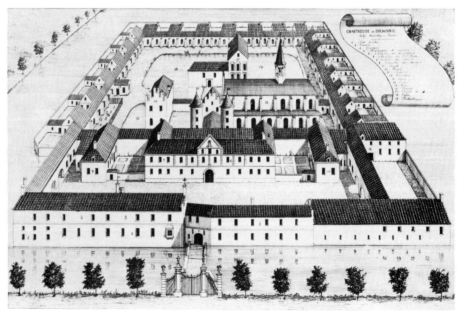

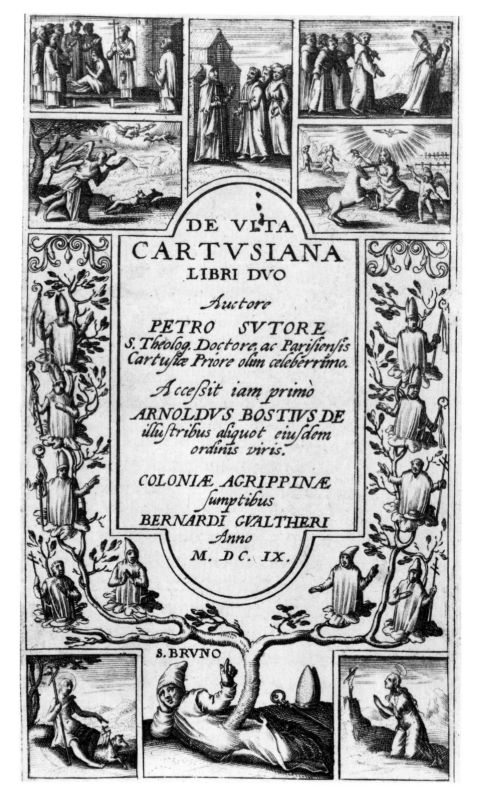

DE VITA
CARTVSIANA
LIBRI DVO

*Auctore*

PETRO SVTORE
*S. Theolog. Doctore, ac Parisiensis
Cartusiæ Priore olim celeberrimo.*

*Accessit iam primò*

ARNOLDVS BOSTIVS DE
*illustribus aliquot eiusdem
ordinis viris.*

COLONIÆ AGRIPPINÆ
*sumptibus*
BERNARDI GVALTHERI
*Anno*
M. DC. IX.

S. BRVNO

*Opposite page:*
93 The title-page of Peter
Sutor's *De Vita Cartusiana*
(1609), from a copy formerly
at Dülmen. *(London Oratory
Library).*

95

servant and useless prior of the same house.' Such detachment from rank and honours is a virtue that Oratorians too have made a special point of cultivating.

Faber was but the most distinguished of the many London Oratorians who have both written and collected books: indeed the majority of the early fathers came into this category—Hutchison, Dalgairns, Knox, Stanton being the most familiar names. For example, Father Antony Hutchison (1822-1863) published in 1863 *Loreto and Nazareth*, a volume of lectures on the Holy House of Loreto. His researches on the subject involved the formation of a comprehensive collection of earlier writing, including two very early and rare publications, Baptista Mantuanus's history of Loreto (1489) and Erasmus's proper for the mass of our Lady of Loreto (1523). This may serve to illustrate how the production of devotional and apologetic works, whether doctrinal or historical, was seen as part of the apostolate of the London Oratory, and that the creation of a great library of Catholic theology and history was seen as an essential precondition for this. It is striking how many books the London Oratorians managed to produce, despite an avowed policy to give priority to pastoral work; and it is equally remarkable what large sums several of them spent on purchasing books at a time when the overall finances of the house were still insecure.

94 Father Philpin de Rivière. *(London Oratory album)*.

95 Father Sebastian Bowden. *(London Oratory album)*.

**XIII** *Moses and the Burning Bush,* from a fifteenth century Rouen Book of Hours. *(London Oratory Library).*

XIV *The Annunciation* from a fifteenth century Troyes Book of Hours. *(London Oratory Library).*

Of all the fathers who contributed to the library collection, the greatest single donor was a member of the generation subsequent to that of Faber and his companions—Father Ignatius Antrobus (1837-1903). The son of a baronet, he was educated at Eton, where he showed a particular gift for languages, and then entered the diplomatic service; it was while attached to our embassy at Paris that he was received into the Catholic Church. He soon renounced his career as a diplomat, and in 1869 entered the London Oratory. His standing as an indispensable member of the community was affirmed by his twice being elected provost, dying in office in 1903. Father Ralph Kerr, in his *The Oratory in London*, wrote of him in 1930: 'Tall, handsome and courtly, he remained the diplomat to the end of his days, and by his very presence lent dignity to the stately functions at which he assisted; but he will be best remembered, by his community for the unfailing serenity of his remarkably harmonious character, and by all who came into contact with him for the frank, urbane and kindly bearing of a English Catholic gentleman.' The first generation of Oratorians had been more lively than this, in the great creative period of the house; but it was now in its phase of late Victorian consolidation, which saw the building of the great church, and we can appreciate how in this phase solid virtues were more necessary than brilliant ones. But for our purposes it is more pertinent to note that his main interest, outside his priestly duties, was historical reading, in a variety of languages; let us recall that he translated two great Oratorian classics, Bacci's *Life of St Philip* and *The Excellences of the Oratory*, and started the English translation of Pastor's *Lives of the Popes*, later to be

96 Father Ralph Kerr. *(London Oratory album)*.

97 Father Antony Hutchison. *(London Oratory album)*.

97

98 Father Ignatius Antrobus. *(London Oratory album).*

99 David Lewis. *(London Oratory album).*

continued by an Oratorian already mentioned, Fr Ralph Kerr. His own book-collecting was stimulated both by this serious historical interest and by his responsibilities as Father Librarian, a position he held from 1878 till 1901. Clearly a man of some wealth, he gave to the library over the years a rich and wide-ranging collection of 5,791 volumes. From these, three groups may be singled out for mention. First, let us note a large collection of the Church Fathers, including all four hundred volumes of Migne's Patrologies, many other collections by Mansi, Mai, Pitra and others, and many fine folio editions of the seventeenth and eighteenth centuries. Before Father Antrobus the Oratory already possessed some fine volumes in this field, such as the great Benedictine editions of Augustine and John Chrysostom, but the huge collection of Patristica that is now to be seen is largely the work of Father Antrobus. A second area, and one where his contribution is even more dominant, is that of books on Byzantine history and on the Latin Crusader states in Greece and the Near East; here he obtained everything of significance that appeared in his lifetime, including forty-nine volumes of the Bonn Corpus of Byzantine historians and the sixteen volumes of the *Recueil des historiens des croisades*. Thirdly, we may note a fine collection, probably unequalled in England, of material on Jansenism and its French environment; this includes a complete run of *Nouvelles Ecclésiastiques* (1728-1789), the 1775 edition in forty-nine volumes of the works of

Arnauld, and the original thirteen volumes, in a fine binding with the royal arms of France, of *Gallia Christiana* (1716-1785). In all, the emphasis in the Oratory Library on patristics and church history, despite strengths in other areas, remains as the legacy of the historical interests and wide linguistic competence of this the greatest of the Father Librarians; and this legacy is an appropriate one, since it is in the Oratorian tradition to concentrate on history rather than on the more controversial area of dogmatic theology.

So far we have followed the building up of the library by the Oratory fathers themselves, and indeed by far the greater part of the collection was made by them. However, there have over the years been gifts by some distinguished benefactors. In 1851 Pope Pius IX gave the fourteen volumes of Schmalzgrueber's *Ius Ecclesiasticum Universum;* in 1869 the Duke of Norfolk gave a fine copy of the London Polyglott Bible of 1657; in 1881, as mentioned above, Cardinal Newman gave a complete set of his works. One notable benefaction, from a less brilliant name, was the gift by one Arthur Coombs in 1866 and 1870 of two illuminated Books of Hours; one of these, a Rouen Book of Hours of the end of the fifteenth century, has singularly attractive and unusual illustrations, including the delectably pastoral *Moses and the burning bush* reproduced in this volume, and twelve exquisite vignettes for major feasts of the year.

However, such gifts have not been numerous; and only two benefactors from outside the house have made substantial gifts. One of these was the hymnologist Orby Shipley, who gave the library four hundred volumes between 1880 and his death in 1916; thereafter his widow gave the library a further five hundred volumes from her husband's collection. Alongside miscellaneous volumes on a disconcertingly wide range of subjects, secular as well as ecclesiastical, we find many books on liturgy and an interesting group of Recusant publications. The Oratory collection of Recusant literature may be introduced here. Unlike most of the other collections we have mentioned, it is not largely the work of a single donor, but was built up by numerous fathers. Apart from the usual range of devotional literature, it includes the original contemporary accounts of several martyrdoms, including those of St Thomas More, St Edmund Campion and St Oliver Plunket, and a few of the rare finely printed books, notably Bishop Challoner's *Britannia Sancta* (1745).

The other main external benefactor was the greatest single donor to the whole library—Mr David Lewis. Born in 1814, the same year as Faber, he became, as Fellow of Jesus College, Oxford and curate of St Mary the Virgin's, a close disciple of Newman, whom he followed into the Catholic Church in 1846. Instead of proceeding to orders, in 1849 he married, and adopted the life of what is called a gentleman of leisure; in his case, however, leisure consisted of intensive, uninterrupted reading, habitually ten or eleven hours a day, on the whole range of theology. One field which he made peculiarly his own was that of Canon Law: on this unpopular but important subject he acquired the reputation of an expert and was often consulted, as much outside his own communion as within it. He produced a number of publications, of which the most notable was his translation of the works of St John of the Cross and of St

Teresa; but he gave priority not to writing but to reading, and in the latter found as much contentment as life can offer: he boasted in his eightieth year that, while reading, he had never had a headache, never desired a companion and never felt depressed. Clearly a man of means, he was a patron of the London Oratory from its foundation, accepted as virtually an honorary member of the community, always present with them on St Philip's Day and included in some community photographs. On his death in 1895 the Oratory inherited a large part of his fortune and his whole library, consisting of over ten thousand volumes; since he had been careful not to duplicate the existing Oratory collection, his bequest represented pure expansion. In this 'Lewis Collection', as it is still called, the breadth of his own reading is obviously represented, but certain groups stand out and can be briefly delineated. First, there is predictably a very impressive collection on Canon Law. This includes three long mediaeval manuscripts, of which one (a fourteenth century record of decisions by the Roman Rota) is unique and of real importance; of printed collections of decisions we find more than fifty folio volumes dating to between 1551 and 1730, among which special mention is deserved by a set of Francis Zilettus's great compilation, *Tractatus Universi Iuris*, commissioned by Pope Gregory XIII and published in Venice in 1584. Secondly, in view of the Lewis translation of St John of the Cross and St Teresa, we may note the large collection he built up of editions of their works, going back to 1626, and of secondary literature. Thirdly, the Lewis Collection contains the main part of the library's strength both in mediaeval liturgical manuscripts, ten in number, and in incunabula, amounting to more than seventy publications; of these, the finest manuscript is perhaps the illuminated missal written in about 1450 for the Bishop of Nevers, and the finest incunabulum the four-volume *editio princeps* of the theologian Alexander of Hales, published at Nuremberg in 1482. Finally, among individual rarities, we may single out two exceptionally fine editions of the *Rituale Romanum*, dating to 1516 and 1584: these are items of extreme rarity, since both editions, because of minor defects, were immediately suppressed by order of the pope and largely destroyed. A delightful but accidental acquisition is an album of sketches by Mr Lewis's mother-in-law, Lady Jane Methuen, that includes autographs by Scott, Thomas Moore and Byron, the Byron manuscript being a first draft, much corrected, of *The Vision of Belshazzar*. In all, the Lewis Collection is an impressive monument to the erudition and generosity of a fine representative of a breed that seems extinct in our own meaner century—the gentleman scholar, dedicating his life to learning, without any tinge of personal ambition.

With the Lewis bequest of 1895 and the death of Father Antrobus in 1903, the great period of the creation of the library comes to an end. But the collection has continued to expand, in various ways. First, we may note the continuation of the custom by which fathers give or bequeath rare or at least practical editions to the community library. In 1906, for example, there were incorporated into the library some important volumes from the collection of Father Charles Bowden (1836-1906), including many early editions of the works of Savonarola, the contro-

100 Father Charles Bowden. *(London Oratory album).*

101 Father Michael McKee. *(London Oratory album).*

versial figure to whom St Philip, in loyalty to the Florentine republican tradition, had a special devotion; it was also from the estate of Charles Bowden that came the main part of the collection in the archives of letters by Faber. In the year of the church's centenary, we may note incidentally that it was this same father who was entrusted by the community with supervising the building of the church, and that the finest features in its adornment are due to him: it was he who discovered and negotiated the purchase of the great statues of the twelve Apostles, and who designed, and paid for, the decoration of St Wilfrid's Chapel.

But of all the members of the community since Father Antrobus who have contributed to the library the outstanding donor was Father Michael McKee. Born in 1865, and then an Anglican clergyman, he entered the Oratory in 1904, where he died in 1927 as the result of being run down by a cyclist. His favourite sphere of activity appears to have been the library, of which he was in charge for most of his priestly life; he contributed regularly to the Catholic press, but in the parish itself was one of the least known of the fathers. However, within the community, and among those parishioners who got through his retiring façade, he was valued, we are told, as an extraordinarily attractive personality, with a gift of wit and a strong sense of humour. Over the years he gave 820 volumes to the library, and to these were added 494 after his death. His purchases consisted largely of current publications, of unequal interest; but his gifts to the library included some rarities, notably a total of seventy-five Jansenist publications, including many rare pamphlets. Of external benefactors, mention has already been made of Orby Shipley, gifts from whose collection started in the nineteenth century but reached a climax in the 1910s.

A perceptive reader of these pages may have noticed that no mention has been made of purchases by the community as a whole; and certainly, just as the furnishing of the library was carried out exclusively through the generosity of individual fathers, so, until recently, purchases by the community were insignificant in comparison to gifts from individuals. Since the last war, however, the situation has been reversed, and now community purchases are the main contribution to the maintenance of the library as a working instrument. Mention may be made of the Oratory subscriptions to the massive French encyclopedias that have been coming out in fascicles for many years—*Dictionnaire d'Histoire et de Géographie Ecclésiastiques, Dictionnaire de la Bible (Supplément), Dictionnaire de Théologie Catholique, Dictionnaire de Spiritualité, Dictionnaire de Droit Canonique, Dictionnaire d'Archéologie Chrétienne et de Liturgie.*

However, the attention of the community has been directed in this century as much to the arrangement and care of the library as to fresh acquisitions. The present card catalogue was largely compiled by Father McKee in the 1910s: apart from listing all books by author, it includes a subject catalogue. The arrangement of books on the shelves was radically revised by the lay brother Vincent Hayles, who assisted in the library till his death in 1936; there is now in most of the library a rough arrangement according to subject matter, although some sections remain a browser's paradise of the unexpected and unpredictable. The revision of the catalogue that this necessitated was a lengthy operation, gradually carried out by generations of novices and completed in 1962. Since then, much time has been spent, initially by novices and more recently by lay helpers, on cleaning and treating the leather bindings; fortunately, great care was taken to repair and renew bindings when the collection was originally made, and most of them are still in excellent condition. The visual appearance of the library, with its handsome proportions, fine fittings and recently cleaned bindings is beautiful and memorable.

Finally, one general question must be frankly raised: to what extent has the Oratory Library over the years been a working tool, and to what extent a mere antiquarian collection of unread and unreadable tomes? We have noted already that some of the particular collections, such as those of Faber on spirituality, of Hutchison on Loreto, of David Lewis on St John of the Cross and St Teresa, were built up specifically as the tools for writing and translation; and we saw how other collections, such as those of David Lewis on Canon Law and of Father Antrobus on eastern Christian history, arose from a genuine passion for erudition. Therefore we can firmly assert that the Oratory Library was not at all built up by men who were keener to acquire old books than to read them. Of course, a collection originally made by an enthusiast can easily accumulate dust after his death; but the Oratory Library, quite apart from its use by the fathers, remains a recognized contribution to the learned resources of London: in recent years, scholars from home and abroad have visited the library to catalogue its mediaeval manuscripts and incunabula, to hunt in its archives, to consult the Oratorian section and the David Lewis collection on Canon Law. It is the keen wish of such visitors that the library should not be neglected or dispersed; and it may be hoped that the present essay may stimulate further interest among scholars and bibliophiles.

102 Early eighteenth century binding with the insignia of Placidus II Seitz, Abbot of Ettal, Bavaria (1709-36). *(London Oratory Library)*.

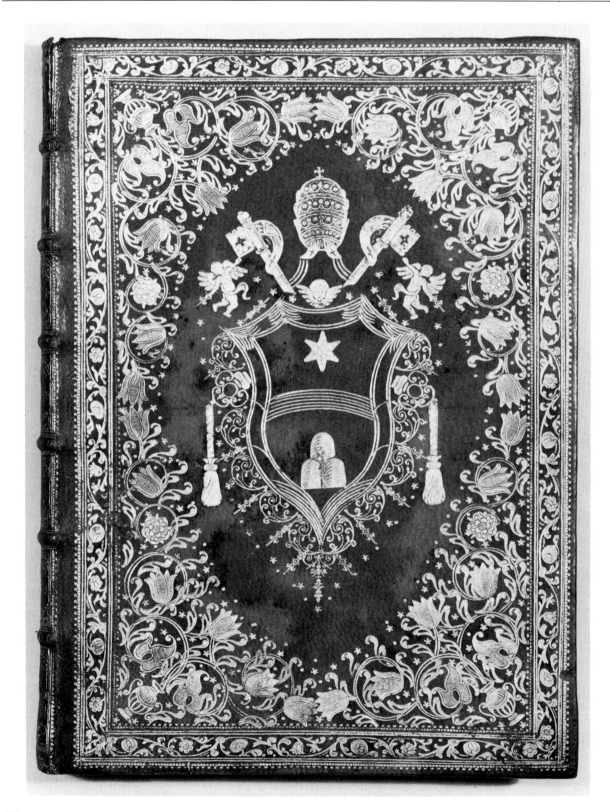

103 Early eighteenth century Italian binding with the arms of Pope Clement XI (1700–21). *(London Oratory Library)*.

104 A fine Roman binding of the *Life of St Philip,* early eighteenth century (*London Oratory* Library).

# THE TREASURY

## *Anna Somers Cocks*

When, in choosing the style of their new church at Brompton, the Oratorian Fathers had specified *Italian Renaissance,* there was nothing to tell them precisely what kind of church plate they should have. There were a number of broad categories available: old continental gothic, old continental baroque and rococo, continental neo-classical, and contemporary—either neo-gothic or 'other' (this last often being a stylistic mongrel, such as, for example the Garrard monstrance, cat. no. 36). In fact, the Oratory's treasury today consists predominantly of the second category, the baroque and rococo. Common-sense indicated that this was the most appropriate for a baroque-style church, and indeed it must have been a deciding factor, if Fr Faber and his successors ever hesitated in making their choice. But equally important must have been the off-putting fanatical behaviour of Augustus Welby Pugin in the gothic-versus-classicism row which raged in the late 1840s.

Pugin was the brilliant but slightly mad prophet of the Gothic Revival, an ardent convert to Catholicism, and one who endowed his own views on the appropriateness of the gothic style to places of worship with the quality of infallibility. He believed that not only should a church be mediaeval in appearance, but also the vestments and liturgical vessels.[1] If he had had his way he would even have re-introduced the early mediaeval liturgical dove hoisted above the altar for the reservation of the Blessed Sacrament, and he tried to make the priests in his churches wear the mediaeval chasuble (which, incidentally, has become quite common since the Second Vatican Council) instead of the short fore-and-aft style in use at the time. The period of church goldsmithing which he admired most was that of thirteenth and fourteenth century Italy—of Assisi, Perugia, Arezzo and Cortona.[2] The style which he abominated was that of baroque Rome. In March 1847, while travelling in Italy, he wrote, 'I have now seen Rome and what Italian architecture can do, and I do not hesitate to say that it is an imperative duty on every Catholic to defend true and Christian architecture with his whole energy. The modern churches here are frightful: St Peter's is far more ugly than I expected, and vilely constructed'. To Lord Shrewsbury he even wrote, 'I do not despair of St Peter's being rebuilt in a better style'.[3]

He was outraged by Fr Faber and his Oratorians opening the Lowther rooms as a chapel in 1849—'a place for the vilest debauches, masque-rades etc.—one night a MASQUE BALL, next BENEDICTION ...I give the whole Order up for ever'.[4] He was bitterly disappointed to hear that they were not intending to build their new Oratory in the gothic style, and when, according to Faber, he 'cursed the Oratory', Newman clearly thought that Pugin had gone too far and wrote a most reasonable, if teasing letter to his friend, Ambrose Phillipps, pointing out ·' at Pugin was more likely to drive people into supporting Italian architecture than not, and that people, 'will not be put down without authority which is infallible. And if we go to authority I suppose Popes have given greater sanction to Italian art that to Gothic'.[5]

As Newman said, this was not the way to win people over, and it is not surprising that thereafter Faber avoided anything to do with Pugin and his Gothic Revival. But this had not always been so: Faber had started out with a great admiration for the gothic, which is recorded in his writings from when he visited France in 1843—St Ouen in Rouen in particular, made a great impression on him. When, in 1846, he gathered together his little community of St Wilfrid's in Colmore Terrace, Pugin designed the altar for the drawing room adapted to a chapel. That same year the Wilfridians moved to Cotton Hall, which had been given them by Lord Shrewsbury, who also largely financed a church for them, again designed by Pugin. To furnish this, Fr Faber turned to the most important ecclesiastical metalworkers of the time, John Hardman & Co., who favoured the gothic style[6]. This Catholic Birmingham firm, founded in 1838, advertised the following years in the *Laity's Directory,* that it was producing from Pugin's designs, 'and with scrupulous regard for canonical laws'. Fr Faber's purchases were not lavish, but they included, in 1847, a gilt chalice and paten at ten guineas, a portable altar, two zinc and gilded processional lanterns at £6.10s., a small plated lamp and chains at £3, and a large brass basin at 11s.6d. In June 1849 he bought, among other things, a round brass corona lamp and another wrought-iron corona for eight lights.[7]

These pieces, if they still survive, are not at the Brompton Oratory today, and nothing more was bought from Hardman's after the move to London, no doubt partly because of its close association with Pugin.

Unfortunately, no record was kept of where the collection of plate at the Oratory was bought. Many of the pieces were gifts; for example, the handsome gold chalice by Ramsden & Carr, presented to Fr Digby Best on his Golden Jubilee in 1908 (cat. no. 17); or acquisitions by individual members of the Community, in particular the chalices. The large nineteenth century French monstrance (cat. no. 37) incorporates, among other jewels, an 1830s parure of pink topazes and pearls, all presented, following time-honoured tradition, by devout women of the parish. It is reasonable to assume that the contemporary pieces, such as the Garrard's monstrance of 1849 (cat. no. 36), and the Hunt & Roskell gold chalice of 1861 (cat. no. 15), were acquired directly from the makers shortly after the date of manufacture.

But we can only guess at how the antique plate came to be in the collection. Apart from the antique dealers proper, many retail silversmiths such as Lambert & Rawlings dealt in old silver. It is also possible that priests from the Oratory brought pieces back from abroad.

A great deal of church plate was on the market, mostly because of the suppression of religious houses and the French Revolution. The

Enlightenment and the new liberal economic thought of the eighteenth century made governments hostile to the Church's huge holdings of property, and in country after country these were confiscated. In the Hapsburg Empire between 1782 and 1786 Joseph II suppressed 783 religious houses. In France the closing-down of religious institutions began under Louis XV, but the Revolution from 1792 onwards completed the process most thoroughly.[8] In Germany, of the 1500 Benedictine monasteries which had existed in the fifteenth century, less than thirty survived the Napoleonic period, and amongst those suppressed were thousand-year old foundations such as St Emmeram in Regensberg, Tegernsee, Wessobrunn, Benediktbeuern and Ottobeuren. And after 1830 the more liberal regimes in Europe were again dissolving religious houses. Libraries, furnishings, art treasures were dispersed, and tons of plate melted down. Some, however, was released on to the art market, to be bought by the growing number of collectors interested in the decorative arts.

This great upheaval in the Church doubtless lies behind the Oratory's possession of so much fine German silver: for example, the gem-set rococo cruets and chalice (cat. no. 13) made in Munich for a Cistercian foundation; the seventeenth-century Augsburg candlesticks (cat. nos. 26 & 27) from Kreuzlingen in Switzerland, suppressed in 1848; and the exquisite rococo cruets (cat. no. 22) made in Bolzano for a Tyrolese shrine.

The other important group in the treasury is of late seventeenth and early eighteenth century Utrecht silver. This includes two pairs of candlesticks (cat. nos. 24 & 25), a large set of dummy vases (cat. nos. 30, 31 & 32), and a showy four-foot high monstrance surround (cat. no. 33).

Despite the 1581 law prohibiting the practising of the Catholic faith in Utrecht, it nonetheless flourished, and quite considerable amounts of church silver were made in the late seventeenth and eighteenth centuries. Here there were no dissolutions; rather the re-establishment of the hierarchy in 1853 led to grand new churches being built, and old unwanted plate being sold off. It is likely that the Oratory bought all its pieces, perhaps from one source, thereafter.

Fortunately, the Oratory was not in competition for purchases with its growing neighbour, the South Kensington Museum (now the V & A). The museum favoured old gothic, or Renaissance plate, and partly because of its interest, prices were rising fast: £16 for a fifteenth century cup from the Basle cathedral treasury in 1855; £122 for another with the same origin in 1861.[9] The museum was enough in Pugin's camp to despise rococo and baroque, and, since there cannot have been many other buyers in the market, the Oratory probably acquired its pieces relatively cheaply, perhaps more cheaply than if it had gone to Hardman's for new work.

So, when Cardinal Newman gave a chalice to the newly completed Oratory for its consecration in 1884, it was a late seventeenth century German baroque example which he chose (cat. no. 5), and he was contributing to the best collection of continental baroque and rococo church plate in the country.

NOTES

1 See A. W. N. Pugin, *Glossary of ecclesiastical ornament and costume, compiled and illustrated from ancient authorities and examples,* London, 1844, in which all kinds of ecclesiastical furnishings and other objects used in a church are described, with a discussion of their mediaeval antecedents.
2 D. Gwynn, *Lord Shrewsbury, Pugin, and the Catholic Revival,* London, 1944, p. 200. See his letter to Lord Shrewsbury praising the Gothic shrine reliquaries and chalices.
3 *Ibid.,* pp. 199-200.
4 *Ibid.,* p. 122.
5 *Ibid.,* p. 121.
6 *Victorian Church Art,* exhibition catalogue, London, Victoria & Albert Museum, 1971, p. 79.
7 Hardman records, Birmingham City Art Gallery and Reference Library, 1845-49, pp. 213, 215, 221, 224. I am most grateful to Mrs Shirley Bury for giving me these references.
8 M. Heimbucher, *Die Orden und Kongregationen der Katholischen Kirche,* reprinted, Paderborn, 1965, I, pp. 246-254.
9 A. Somers Cocks, 'An Episode in Collecting Tastes: German silver at the V & A', *Connaissance des Arts,* January, 1982, pp. 44-51.

105  (Cat. no. 1) Reliquary altar cross. Brussels, 1648-9.

CATALOGUE

**1** *ALTAR CROSS*

Ebony and stained fruitwood, mounted with silver and set with a foiled crystal.
H. 105 cm (3 ft 5½ ins).
Flemish. Town mark of Brussels; date letter: a crowned O, for 1648-49.[1]
The crowned lion rampant—the second and older town mark of Brussels—apparently wanting, as also any maker's mark.
Condition: two relics wanting.
Set in the base, a boxwood carving of the Virgin and Child, with, on either side, miniature paintings of the Virgin and St John. The cross and base set with relics, each identified. In the base: St Albert, illegible, St Lawrence, St Luke, St Peter, St Philip, St Barnabas, St Bernard (?), St Margaret, illegible, wanting, St Alexander, and (the most prominent), the Eleven Thousand Virgins. In the cross: wanting, St Mary Magdalen, illegible, the Blood of St Charles Borromeo.
The finials of the cross-arms embossed and chased with putto-heads, restrained acanthus, husks, and with S-scroll borders. The corpus of cast silver. The volutes at the sides of the base crowned by acanthus finials.

*The combination of ebony or ebonised wood with silver or gold mounts was invented in the important South German goldsmithing centres of Nuremberg and Augsburg in the 1570's (see for example the large house-altar of Duke Albrecht V of Bavaria, made c. 1574, and the contemporary ebony and enamelled gold altarcross, both in the Schatzkammer of the Residenz, Munich.)[2] By the early seventeenth century most small South German reliquaries were black and silver. Relics were nearly always displayed so that they could be seen through little windows, sometimes combined with embroidery or silver wire in decorative patterns, often identified by small curls of paper. Particularly in Spain, small crosses of this type were made of precious metals so that a multiplicity of relics coud be worn on the person.[3] Although the style of this piece ultimately derives from South Germany, it must be remembered that ebony was also much used in Flanders at this time for cabinet making.*

NOTES
**1** Cf. *Orfèvrerie au Poinçon de Bruxelles,* exhibition, 29 rue Ravenstein, Brussels, September-November 1979, Cat. nos. 17 & 18, with the same date letter.
**2** *Official Guide to the Schatzkammer of the Munich Residenz,* Munich, 1970, nos. 59 & 66, respectively.
**3** Eg. Inv. no. M.538-1910, Victoria & Albert Museum.

106 Two chalices. *Left* (Cat. no. 2): French, *c*.1675. Maker's mark: Crowned *IF* with a fleurs-de-lys. *Right* (Cat. no. 3): Aix-en-Provence, *c*.1675. Maker's mark: *AE* below a fleurs-de-lys. The bowl nineteenth century.

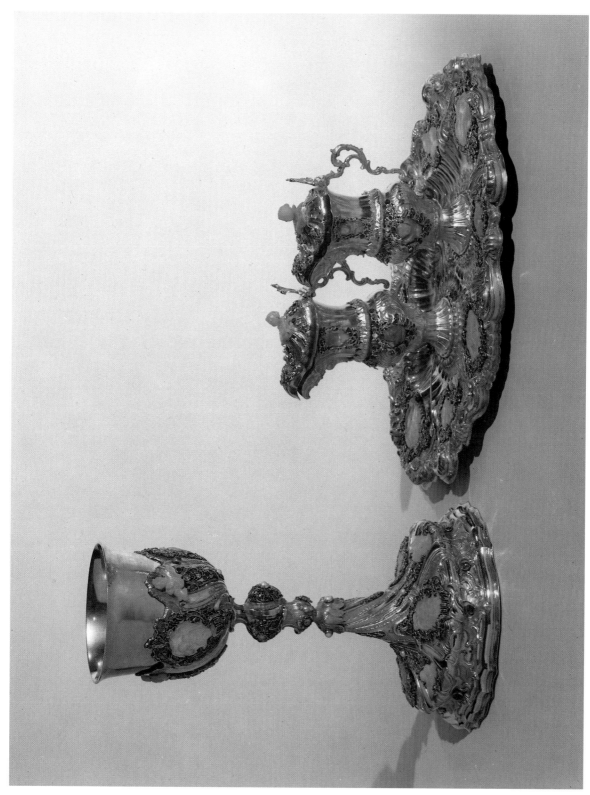

XV The Ellice set. Chalice and cruet. Munich. The chalice c.1752, probably by Johann Michael Roth. The cruets and dish, 1752, probably by Johann Georg Schuster.

XVI Monstrance. French, mid nineteenth century. Maker's mark *CT*. Adorned with jewellery given by members of the congregation.

## 2 *CHALICE*

Silver-gilt.
H. 26.5 cm (10⅜ ins).
French. The maker's mark a crowned *DF* with *fleur-de-lys* and *grains de remède*, twice over and indistinctly; a date letter *Q*; a third mark illegible; *c.*1675.
Condition: regilt by the mercury process, a little worn.
The footrim circular with a pierced egg-and-leaf moulding. A ring of beading above. The foot itself plain, but engraved with a cross. Embossed and chased acanthus leaves descending on to the foot. A ring of beading at top and bottom of stem. The cast oval knop with acanthus leaves, and putto-heads and swags of fruit in between. The bowl fitting into a calyx of acanthus leaves.

*This and cat. no. 3 are typical French chalices of the second half of the seventeenth century. The construction of the shallow plain foot, with its attached convex rim moulding and the deep acanthus calyx are characteristic features.*

## 3 *CHALICE*

Silver gilt.
H. 24 cm (9⅝ ins).
French. Town mark of Aix-en-Provence (a crowned *P* over *AIX*) *c.*1675; maker's mark *AE* below a *fleur-de-lys* unidentified. The bowl with a nineteenth century English maker's mark, *ISH* below a crown.
Condition: the bowl a nineteenth century replacement; the gilding on the stem and foot original and very worn.
The broad convex foot rim cast with a spaced-out gadrooned border. The foot plain, engraved with a cross on a mount,. The moulding separating foot from stem, and stem from bowl, repeating the footrim motif. The knop cast with an acanthus-leaf calyx, and cherub-wings with clusters of fruit in between; the cherub-heads separately applied. The bowl in keeping with the style of the other parts, with a calyx of layered acanthus. Engraved on the underside of the foot: *D.O.M: B.M.V: ET S. EVTROPIO.M.GRATI. ANIMI. SIGNUM. DIE. X OCTOBRIS AD. MD.CCCLIX.* The *AE* and *fleur-de-lys* maker's mark has been identified as being that of Antoine II Escavard (fl. 1581–*c.*1628)[1] but it cannot be so in this case as the chalice must be later on stylistic grounds. (Cf. no. 2).

NOTE
**1** R. Jourdan Barry, *Les Orfèvres de la généralité d'Aix-en-Provence*, Paris, 1974, P. 104.

107  The Newman chalice. (Cat. no 5). German, *c*.1690.

**4** *CHALICE*

Silver gilt.
H. 28 cm (10⅞ ins).
Flemish. Town mark of Antwerp; the date letter probably for 1668; maker's mark only partially stamped, and unidentified.
Condition: regilt.
The hexafoil foot rim embossed with a scrolling ring against a matted ground. The swelling foot prominently embossed with cherubim-heads alternating with putti seated in clouds, holding the symbols of the Passion.
The large oval knop embossed with saints in cartouches: St Catherine, a nun in ecstasy (probably St Teresa of Avila) and St Joseph. A beaded moulding at the top of the stem, and the corolla embossed with putti gambolling among vines.

**5** *THE NEWMAN CHALICE*

Silver-gilt with silver decoration.
H. 27 cm (10½ ins).
German *c*.1690. The marks illegible.
Condition: much worn; the gilding original.
Inscribed under the foot rim: *Fratribus Londinensibus suis, Templum novum et splendidissimum Iam nunc introeuntibus in memoriam rei Ioan. H. Card. Newman.* (John Henry Cardinal Newman gives this to his London brethren in memory of their entering now into their new and most splendid church).
The swelling trefoil foot embossed and chased with the Annunciation, the Nativity and the Assumption of the Virgin. In between are tight acanthus leaves arranged in addorsed C-scrolls, with beading down the centres. The baluster-shaped knop embossed with acanthus. The bowl with a pierced silver corolla of twisting scrolling foliage, and three groups of the symbols of the Passion inside wreaths.

*There are a number of Baroque chalices made in Cologne which similarly combine embossed pictorial scenes with a profusion of acanthus and scrollwork: for example, one by J. Rütgers, of about 1710, with scenes from the Life of Christ (Cologne, parish church of St Gereon.)[1]*
*There had been an unfortunate misunderstanding between Newman at the Birmingham Oratory and the fathers of the London Oratory, who had invited him to the ceremonial opening of the great new church at Brompton on 25 April 1884. Cardinal Newman had demurred over accepting, fearing, in his humility, that by his presence he would be claiming a position of authority over both foundations. This was not comprehended by the Duke of Norfolk, who had issued the invitation, and after a confusing and painful exchange of letters, Newman wrote, 'Alas, alas, why did I not confine myself to the true and sufficient reason that I was too old, too infirm, too worn in mind to leave home? …I have written to Fr Gordon to ask his Fathers to accept from me an offering for their new church'[2] The offering was this chalice.*

NOTES
1 *Rheinische Goldschmiedekunst der Renaissance und Barockzeit* exh. cat. Rheinisches Landesmuseum, Bonn, 1975, no. 51, ill. 43.
2 M. Trevor, *Newman, Light in Winter*, London, 1962, p. 613.

**6** *CHALICE*

Silver-gilt with silver decoration.

H. 24 cm (9½ ins).

German. Town mark of Augsburg for 1690-95 (Seling 146); maker's mark of Johann Joachim I Lutz (Seling 1827b), a Catholic goldsmith who became a master in about 1687, was assay-master between 1711 and 1715, and died in 1727.

Condition: good. The gilding original.

The flaring hexafoil foot embossed and chased with putto-heads, with swags of fruit above them, and acanthus leaves descending from the stem. In between are inset oval silver, medallions embossed with the Agony in the Garden, Christ before Caiaphas, and the Last Supper. The knop cast with blank oval medallions between acanthus leaves. The pierced silver calyx consists of putti and acanthus, with, in between, gilt oval medallions of the Carrying of the Cross, the Crucifixion and the Entombment.

*Johann Joachim I Lutz was one of the most prolific Augsburg goldsmiths, specialising in work for the Catholic churches of Southern Germany right into Central Europe. Many of his pieces are still in situ: there is, for example, a very showy 83 cm. high gem-set monstrance of about 1690 in the parish church, Hilpoltstein; a 133 cm. high silver-gilt statue of the Madonna, c.1700, in the parish church of St Vitus, Ellwangen, and a silver-gilt chalice of about 1708-10 in St Nikolaus, Pleinfeld.*[1]

NOTE
**1** H. Seling, *Augsburger Goldschmiede,* Munich, 1981, III, p. 262.

**7** *THE ARGYLL CHALICE*

Silver-gilt with silver decoration.

H. 23 cm (9 ins).

German *c*.1700. No town mark visible; maker's mark semi-effaced, but possibly that of Jonas Laminit (Seling 1560), a Protestant goldsmith of Augsburg, master in 1550, died 1690.

Condition: a reinforcing rim soldered to the underside of the foot. Regilt.

There are putti embossed on the foot, with bandwork forming C-scrolls in between. A silver band between the stem and the cast knop, with oval medallions and acanthus leaves. The bowl with a silver embossed and pierced calyx of putti and bandwork. The foot inscribed '*A. BENEDICTO CUMBERLEGE. CONG. ORAT. LONDINENSIS D.D. ANNA DUCESSA DE ARGYLL Feb^r XXVIII MDCCCLXIII*' (Ann, Duchess of Argyll gave this to Arthur Benedict Cumberlege of the London Congregation of the Oratory 23rd February 1863). This was given before Fr Cumberlege was ordained, but just after he had completed his three-year probation.

*Ann, Duchess of Argyll, widow of the 7th Duke, was a considerable benefactress of the London Oratory, who, among other things, supplied the rare woods in 1858 for the splendid inlaid floor of the first church (now in the sanctuary), and in 1854 had founded a choir school at a cost of £800. She died in 1874.*

*Although Laminit was a Protestant, it is not impossible that he made this chalice: in Augsburg, Catholic and Protestant goldsmiths occasionally made pieces for churches of the other communion, although goldsmiths who produced large quantities of plate for Catholic churches such as Johann Joachim I Lutz (see no. 6) were always Catholic.*[1]

NOTE

**1** S. Rathke-Koehl, *Geschichte des Augsburger Goldschmiedegewerbes vom Ende des 17. bis zum Ende des 18. Jahrhunderts,* Augsburg, 1964.

108 Two chalices. *Left* (Gat. no. 7): the Argyll chalice. German, *c*.1700. Possibly Augsburg and by Jonas Laminit. *Right* (Cat. no. 6): Augsburg, 1690-95, by Johann Joachim I Lutz.

109 Two chalices. *Left* (Cat. no. 8): Flemish (?) *c.*1710. Maker unidentified. *Right* (Cat. no. 4): Antwerp, 1668 (?). Maker unidentified.

**8** *CHALICE*

Silver-gilt.
H. 27.5 cm (10⅞ ins).
Flemish (?), about 1710. Town mark and maker's mark illegible; *S* in an oval, struck twice.
Condition: the gilding original.
The broad concave foot rim cast and chased with a 'buckler' and dart pattern against a matted ground. The foot plain with embossed and chased acanthus leaves descending on to it from the stem, the base of which is gadrooned. The cast knop waisted, with a gadrooned moulding below and palmettes above. The upper moulding with short acanthus leaves separated by flutes. A gadrooned moulding on the stem above and the deep calyx formed as a tangle of vine leaves and grapes against a matted ground.

*The greater height of this chalice, its weightiness, the gadrooned moulding, and the shape of the knop all suggest a date in the early eighteenth century and the influence of French Régence models. On the other hand, the vine-leaf calyx remains a baroque detail.*

**9** *THE HARRISON CHALICE*

Silver-gilt. Set with enamelled plaques.
H. 27 cm (16⅞ ins).
German. Town mark for Augsburg in use in 1719-20 (Seling 179); maker's mark of Johann David Saler (Seling 1877), a Catholic goldsmith, who became a master in 1693, was assay-master 1707-11 and 1719-23, and died in 1729.
Inscribed: '*Herbertus Harrison in Cong. ingressus die junii XXVI A.D. MDCCCLXI obiit die Junii XVIII A.D. MDCCCLXVII R.I.P.*' (Herbert Harrison entered the Congregation 26 June 1861, died 18 June 1867 R.I.P.)
Condition: the gilding original.
The plaques on the bowl represent St Joseph, the Virgin, and St John; on the foot, St James of Compostella, St Thomas Aquinas, and St Francis.

*Augsburg silver was frequently ornamented with small painted enamel plaques from the last quarter of the seventeenth century onwards. While this kind of 'fire painting', as it was called, had more in common with the art of miniature-painting or ceramic decoration, the goldsmiths' guild still tried to guard its old prerogative of executing it. In reality, however, only a few goldsmiths practised it, and the small plaques were often bought from independent specialised craftsmen.[1]*
*Saler clearly worked predominantly for the Catholic church and numerous pieces by him survive, often in the places for which they were made: eg. a silver parcel-gilt cruet set c. 1708-10, engraved with the Imperial eagle (Vienna, Geistliche Schatzkammer); statue of the Virgin, silver and parcel-gilt, set with gems, c.1729-30, H. 85.5 cm. (Grand Séminaire Catholique, Strasbourg); chalice,*

110 Two chalices. *Left* (Cat. no. 9): the Harrison chalice. Augsburg, 1719-20, by Johann David Saler. *Right* (Cat. no. 10): set with gem-stones and enamel medallions. Augsburg, 1719-20, by Johann Caspar Lutz.

*silver-gilt, c.1737-39, H. 26 cm. (Catholic parish church of Maria Himmelfahrt, Landsberg-am-Lech)*[2].

NOTES
1 S. Rathke-Koehl, *Geschichte des Augsburger Goldschmiedegewerbes vom Ende des 17. bis zum Ende des 18. Jahrhunderts,* Augsburg, 1964.
2 Seling, vol, III, p. 227.

## 10 *CHALICE*

Silver–gilt, with six painted enamel plaques in silver settings studded with garnets, amethysts and rock crystals. The plaques on the bowl represent: The Last Supper, Gethsemane, and The Scourging; on the foot: the Crowning with Thorns, the Carrying of the Cross, and the Crucifixion.

German. Town mark of Augsburg for 1719-20 (Seling 179); maker's mark of Johann Caspar Lutz (Seling 2086), son of Johann Joachim I Lutz (see no. 6), a Catholic like his father, and a silverworker; master in 1716, died 1748.

Condition: the plaques perhaps slightly later additions as the embossed decoration continues beneath them. The gilding original.

The silver embossed and chased with bandwork, attenuated acanthus, and fields of imbrication with pairs of putto–heads.

H. 27 cm (10¼ ins).

111 Two chalices. *Left* (Cat. no. 11): Augsburg, 1747-49, by Franz Joseph Schneider. *Right* (Cat. no. 12): the Fawcett chalice. Venice, *c.*1745.

**11** *CHALICE*

Silver-gilt.
H. 27.5 cm (10¾ ins).
German. Town mark of Augsburg for 1747-49 (Seling 226); maker's mark of Franz Joseph Schneider (Seling 2122), a Catholic silverworker who became master in 1719, assay-master in 1740-43, and died 1762.
Condition: good; the gilding original.
The steeply rising foot embossed and chased with swirling 'panels', bold flat rococo scrolls, and vestigial bandwork. The calyx repeats this decoration, but with small clusters of naturalistic flowers. A cornice-like roll moulding finishes it off, with a ripple of rocaille encroaching on the smooth bowl. The triangular knop is cast and chased.

*The piece is remarkable for its great elaboration of texture: coarse matting, fine matting, ribbing, dotting, and wavy backgrounds. A silver-gilt chalice by this master, of 1755-57, is in St Emmeram, Regensburg.*

**12** *THE FAWCETT CHALICE*

Silver, parcel-gilt.
H. 28.5 cm (11⅛ ins).
Italian, circa 1745, town mark of Venice; no maker's mark.
Condition: good. The gilding original.
The foot embossed and chased with rococo panelling and asymmetrical leaves on the rim. The foot shows the Virgin, Matthew, Mark and John. The shaped knop cast and chased with flowers and foliage, scrolls, and asymmetrical leaves. The calyx embossed with the Virgin and Child, St Anthony of Padua, a male saint with a set square, and a cleric with one hand on a book, the other holding a lily. A plaque inset in the base is engraved: *ALTARI S. WILFRIDI ANNA FAWCETT D.D.D. 1884.*

## 13 *CHALICE AND CRUETS (THE ELLICE SET)*

Silver-gilt, set with carved mother-of-pearl plaquettes, pearls, garnets, emeralds, amethysts and rock crystals.
H. of chalice: 33 cm (13 ins). H. of cruets: 17 cm (6¾ ins).
L. of dish: 41.5 cm (16 ins).
German. Town Mark of Munich.
The chalice: *c*.1752, date mark illegible; maker's mark *MR*, probably of Johann Michael Roth, who became a master in 1745 and died in 1763.[1]
Condition: the gilding original.
The cruets and dish: date mark, 1752, maker's mark probably of Johann Georg Schuster who came to Munich from Grub, in the demesne of the Valley family, was apprenticed to the *Juwelier* Zech in 1736, made free in 1742, and a master of the goldsmiths' guild in 1753. He died in 1776.[2]
Condition: the cruets regilt and their mother-of-pearl plaquettes wanting. The gilding of the dish original.
All parts are in a flamboyant spiralling rocaille. The bowl of the chalice is set with mother-of-pearl plaquettes carved in relief:

a) a monk holding a cross, lance and sponge (St Bernard);
b) an old bearded abbot blessing and looking to heaven, with a book in one hand and on it a beaker, from which emerges a serpent's tail (St Benedict);
c) a monk holding a ring in the right hand (St Robert of Molesme);

On the foot:
d) a monk with a posy of flowers (Bl. Gero of Raitenhaslach?);
e) monk looking heavenward, holding a scroll or stole;
f) a monk (but with a helmet-shaped hat) with a hairshirt and scourge (St William of Aquitaine);

On the dish:
g) A monk preaching with his hand on a skull;
h) a priest in biretta and fur-trimmed mozzetta with open book, shepherd's stone-thrower and sheep (St Wendel?);
i) a monk with his finger in a book;
j) a pope praying, with two doves coming from the sky (St Eugene III).

*The overall design of the cruets and dish is ensuite with the chalice, but the execution is finer, with touches of naturalism in the vines and floral swags, and a greater range of matting, and chased detail.*

*From the 1720s until the 1760s it was quite common for liturgical plate, especially pieces made in South Germany, to be decorated with brightly coloured enamel plaques, or gems set in silver scrollwork. As here, the intrinsic value of the stones is often not high, but the effect is showy and suited to the drama and bright colouring of rococo high altars, where, at the moment of the elevation, the liturgical high-point of the mass, the large and flashing chalice, which could easily be seen by the congregation, was also the culmination of the architectural setting.*

The saints carved on the mother-of-pearl plaquettes, because often with idiosyncratic or undistinctive attributes, have proved remarkably difficult to identify, but the presence of St Bernard and of other saints of, or associated with, the Cistercian order makes it fairly certain that this set of liturgical vessels was made for a Cistercian abbey. St Robert of Molesmes was the actual founder of the Cistercian order, though St Bernard is often wrongly credited with that role. Eugenius III was the first Cistercian to become Pope, and St William of Aquitaine was often confused with William IX, the last Duke of Aquitaine, who was converted by St Bernard. St Benedict laid down the Rule which the Cistercians' was a reformed version. The most unusual figure is the Bl. Gero of Raitenhaslach, who was abbot of the Cistercian abbey of this name in Lower Bavaria; he was handed a three-blossomed rose by a well-wisher to warn him against his assassins.[3] If the identification of this saint is correct, it is very possible that this set of liturgical vessels was originally made for Raitenhaslach (which lost most of its plate when it was dissolved) since his cult was very limited in its diffusion.

Johann Michael Roth was a goldsmith who worked more than once in conjunction with the prominent sculptors of the day. The records of the Theatinerkirche in Munich show that he was called in to finish a rococo frame which had been designed in Paris by the Bavarian court sculptor Wilhelm de Groff, who died. Roth also made a rococo frame designed by the sculptor Johann Baptist Straub, for a painting of the Annunciation by Georges Desmarées, likewise for the Theatinerkirche. In a petition dated 18 July 1762 to the court, presenting his case for being made a court goldsmith, Roth says that he had made a number of other large-scale works: a valuable frame for Kloster Melk, an altar frontal for the shrine at Andechs, the new antipendium for the Theatinerkirche in Munich, and a 'superb, precious' frame for the noble Slav Brotherhood in the same church (which may have been the one designed by de Groff). None of these works survives, but there is a large gem-studded rococo chalice very similar to the one under discussion in the Herzog-Spitalkirche in Munich. This bears the mark IMR. Two pieces, with the MR mark found on the Oratory chalice, can also be attributed to Roth: a large early rococo monstrance with the Pelican in his Piety and God the Father under a baldacchino, of c.1740. H. 98 cm (Parish church of St Nikolaus, Rosenheim), and a richly embosssed rococo chalice, c.1760, H. 32 cm (Parish church, Weyarn, B.A. Miesbach).[4] The making of the cruets and salver must have been farmed out to Johann Georg Schuster, who in 1752 was still one year from being an independent master of the guild. Other pieces with his mark are: a finely embossed silver-gilt rococo ciborium, Munich, 1760 (formerly Allerheiligen Hofkirche, Munich) and a pair of rococo silver cruets and salver, after 1750 (Dreifaltigkeitskirche, Munich).[5]

NOTES
1  M. Frankenburger, *Die Alt-Münchner Goldschmiede und ihre Kunst*, Munich, 1912, p. 406.
2  *op. cit.*, p. 410.
3  I am grateful to Alastair Laing for help with the putative identification of these saints.
4  M. Frankenburger, *op. cit.*, pp. 226, 406-407.
5  *op. cit.*, p. 410.

112 Chalice and paten. (Cat. no. 14). French. The chalice mid nineteenth century, by Garnier; the paten, 1809, maker unidentified.

**14** *CHALICE AND PATEN*

Silver–gilt.

French. The chalice with the standard mark for .950 silver in use from 1838 onwards, and with the maker's mark, Garnier. The paten with the *poinçon de titre* for Paris 1809-17, tax mark for 1809, standard mark 1809-17, goldsmiths' association mark, marker's mark *PP* and two illegible marks. The chalice mid-nineteenth century, the paten 1809. The foot rim engraved *DONNE PAR FRANCOIS BERNEDE A LA CATHEDRALE DE BAYONNE 1650.*

H. 31.5 cm (12¼ ins); diam. of paten 16.5 cm (6½ ins).

Embossed and chased with contrasting textures. The foot with three oval medallions framing the Scourging, the Dicing soldiers, and the Carrying of the Cross, with grapevines in between. The fretted calyx with busts in medallions of Christ, the Virgin, and St John the Evangelist, with ears of corn, grapevines and bullrushes in between. The paten with the Deposition from the Cross on a roundel in the centre.

*The inscription on the foot cannot refer to this particular chalice, which is clearly nineteenth century in date and displays many details of late neo-classicism, such as bands of small stiff ivy leaves, and leaf and dart pattern. It may however record an older chalice which became too fragile for use, and was replaced by this one, perhaps using metal to its value.*

*It was probably acquired in England from Bowler & Jones, jewellers and silver-smiths of 71, Piccadilly, as those are the names on the red morocco case.*

113 Two chalices. *Left* (Cat. no. 15): Sheffield, 1861, by Hunt and Roskell. *Right* (Cat. no. 17): the Digby Best chalice. London, 1908, by Omar Ramsden and Alwyn Carr.

## 15 CHALICE AND PATEN

18 carat gold.
H. 24 cm (9½ ins).
English. Town mark of Sheffield for 1861; maker's mark of Hunt and Roskell.
Condition: good.
The dominant motif on the foot and bowl, anthemion alternating with cherubim-heads. The knop fluted, with a guilloche pattern between the flutes. The base, stem, and corolla semi-matte, the cup burnished.
The paten plain.

*John Samuel Hunt was the nephew of the famous Regency goldsmith Paul Storr, who had brought him into his firm of Storr & Mortimer in the mid 1820s, and trained him as a successor. On Storr's retirement in 1839 the name of the firm changed to Mortimer & Hunt. In 1844 John Mortimer retired, and Robert Roskell went into partnership with Hunt. Storr had earlier in his career worked for Rundell's, the royal goldsmiths, and he transmitted his admiration of their styles to his nephew. Thus Hunt & Roskell extended the life of many designs which dated from the 1820s into the second half of the nineteenth century. At the Great Exhibition of 1851, for example, they gave prominence to the designs of, among others, that great figure of neo-classicism, John Flaxman.[1] This inclination clearly has affected the choice of ornament—anthemion and cherubim-heads—for the chalice under discussion.*

NOTE
1  S. Bury, 'The lengthening shadow of Rundells, Part 2: The substance and growth of the Flaxman tradition', *Connoisseur*, 1966, pp. 157-158.

## 16 THE PURCELL/WOODRUFF CHALICE AND PATEN

Silver–gilt, set with a cabochon cornelian, moonstone, smokey topaz, amethyst and peridot. The base with a diamond cross and an enamelled medallion of the Virgin of the Immaculate Conception. The paten plain.
A green stone set beneath the foot.
H. 21 cm (8¹⁄₁₀ ins).
English. London mark for 1868-9; 'maker's' mark of Lambert & Co., but the corolla stamped with the mark of the actual maker, W. W. Williams, a plateworker who registered his mark in 1860.[1]
Inscribed beneath the foot: *REVERENDO VIRO JACOBO PURCELL MULTARUM EJUS VIRTUTUM EXIMIARUM, ASSIDUITATISQUE PER QUINQUE ANNOS APUD PARKHURST, QUIDAM FAMILIARES HUNC CALICEM (ET HANC PATENAM) DONANT, ET JOHANNES EVELEIGH WOODRUFF MONUMENTUM, UT AD AMICORUM EJUS NUMERUM SEMPER ADSCRIBANTUR, ORANT 28 MARTII MCMXXVI XII KAL: AUG: MDCCCLXIX* (For the Rev. Jacob Purcell, as a monument of his many extraordinary virtues, and of his assiduity for five years at Parkurst, John Eveleigh Woodruff and some familiars give this chalice (and this paten). They pray that they might always be inscribed among the number of his friends. 28 March 1926 XII Kal. Aug. 1869).

*The style is neo-Gothic, imitating French mediaeval models. It is interesting that the two sets of 'maker's' marks appear on the piece because, although it was well known that the retailers who sent in the plate to be marked often had not made the pieces themselves, the use of two maker's marks was not allowed, so the Assay Office must have missed the W.W.W. Fr Purcell was not an Oratorian (he was presumably Chaplain to Parkhurst Prison, on the Isle of Wight), but Fr Woodruff was (ordained in 1912), so the chalice must have been returned to him, perhaps by bequest.*

## 17 *THE DIGBY BEST CHALICE AND PATEN*

Gold, the knop set with cushion-cut garnets, and the underside of the foot with an amethyst, perhaps formerly the bezel of a ring, and with an amethyst and pearl brooch.

H. 25 cm (9¾ ins).

English. The standard mark for nine carat gold; London date letter for 1908-9; maker's mark of Omar Ramsden (1873-1939) and Alwyn Carr (1872-1940) registered in 1898. Inscribed on the base: *Omar Ramsden and Alwyn Carr made me.*

Condition: good.

The hand-raised foot with beading around it, the knop embossed and chased to resemble a cluster of grapes. The calyx chased with art-nouveau 'baroque' shields, on which are the symbols of the Passion, with acanthus leaves inbetween.

Inscribed on the underside of the foot: *Presented to Father Kenelm Digby Best at the Oratory on the attainment of the Golden Jubilee of his priesthood 10 October 1908.*

*The first significant commission in Omar Ramsden's career came in 1897, when he won the first prize in the competition to design a mace for the city of Sheffield, presented by the Duke of Norfolk, the town's first Lord Mayor. To help him execute this, Omar Ramsden went into partnership with Alwyn Carr, and their joint mark was registered in 1898. They also moved to London from Sheffield, their home town. Both were devout Catholics, and the fact that their first important work was executed for the Duke of Norfolk must have helped to bring them important commissions for the Church—1907, for example, the magnificent monstrance for Westminster Cathedral and, indeed, in 1908, this chalice.*

*The business flourished in the years before the First World War, and they took on numerous assistants. In 1919 the partnership broke up, but Ramsden's work-shops grew busier and busier, making numerous ceremonial pieces for universities, City companies, but also private commissions.*

*The artistic tradition to which Ramsden and Carr belonged was the Arts and Crafts one, with an emphasis on the hand-made, often harking back to mediaeval forms, with sinuous, semi-organic ornament, sometimes set with enamelled plaques or cabochon stones.*

*The hand-hammered finish of this piece is typical, and it was indeed labori-ously raised by hand; but, later in his career, many of Ramsden's works were in fact machine-turned for the sake of economy, then briefly hammered over to achieve the same effect – a revealing artistic hypocrisy. This chalice has also adapted some features from continental baroque church plate, with its grape-cluster knop, and shields on the cup with acanthus in between.*

## 18 *MACNAUGHTEN, TUYLL, AND WALPOLE CHALICE AND PATEN*

Silver-gilt, with a diamond-set cross and pearl-set sickle moon on the base.
H. 23.7 cm (9⅕ ins).
English. London mark for 1907-8; maker's mark of Frederick Denby Wray, of 7, Great Sutton Street, Clerkenwell, registered 11th May 1900.
This is an imitation of a seventeenth-century South German chalice type, with large winged putti and grapes on the base, the knop with putto heads and acanthus leaves and the corolla similar, but also with clusters of fruit and marrows.
The paten plain.

*Sidney Blunt and F. D. Wray started a business specialising in ecclesiastical silver in 1888, but the partnership was dissolved in April 1900. F. D. Wray then entered the new mark on his own, but the firm continued under the name of Blunt & Wray. It went into voluntary liquidation c.1931.*[1]

NOTE
[1] I am most grateful to Miss Susan Hare, Librarian at Goldsmiths' Hall, for the elucidation of this mark and the information about the firm.

## 19 *CATOR CHALICE*

Silver.
H. 27 cm (10⅝ ins).
English. Town mark of London for 1911-12; maker's mark of the Goldsmiths' and Silversmiths' Co., Ltd.
Condition: good.
The octofoil foot-rim with putto-heads in the projecting segments. The circular foot embossed and chased with St John the Apostle, St Philip Neri, the Virgin, and St Anselm, in roundels, with grapes in between combined with C-scrolls. The knop cast and chased with grapes and acanthus, while the calyx displays the symbols of the Passion with putti and Edwardian ribbons in between. The foot inscribed: '*Henrico Guglielmo Cator ex grato animo donavit EL 4 June 1887 4 June 1912.*'

*At the time when the chalice was commissioned, the Goldsmiths' and Silversmiths' Company was one of the largest commercial plate manufactories in the country.*

*The chalice copies French examples of the first half of the seventeenth century, in particular the circular foot on a many-lobed rim (cf. the Paris chalice of 1633-4 with this feature, in the Victoria and Albert Museum. M39-1967).*

114 Chalice. (Cat. no. 20).
London, 1931, by Charles
Boyton.

**20** *CHALICE*

Silver, the interior of the bowl gilt.
H. 18.9 cm (7⅜ ins).
English. London date letter for 1931-2; maker's mark of Charles Boyton & Sons; also signed. The mark registered 1904; between World Wars I and II the firm had a shop in Wigmore Street, and the firm closed down shortly before 1939.
The tall hexagonal flaring foot with a closely stepped edge, and a cross engraved on one facet. Applied ribs descend on to the facets from the compressed circular knop which is profiled above and below its diameter. The hemispherical bowl hand-raised with a hammered surface. The underside of the foot rim engraved: *HUNC CALICEM CAROLO KENNEY DEDIT AMICO J B HOLLAND CONG. ORAT. PRESB. 3 JUL. 1932* (J B Holland a priest of the Congregation of the Oratory gave this chalice to his friend Charles Kenney, 3 July 1932).

*Charles Boyton & Sons were a prolific firm with a large range of reproduction and cheap traditional silver. At some time in the 1920s, however, they began to make pieces, as Boyton said, to 'contemporary designs of his own'. Their style, however, remained closer to the surviving Arts and Crafts tradition, with its 'hand-made' look and archaistic forms, than to truly contemporary styles.*

*The Goldsmiths' Company, London, has a goblet of 1931 by Boyton, with a hammered surface, and cast grape and vine decoration of the knop reminiscent of the work of Georg Jensen.*

**21** *CIBORIUM*

Silver, parcel-gilt with silver decoration.
H. 43 cm (17 ins).
German. Town mark of Augsburg for 1698 (Seling 156); maker's mark of Johann Melchior III Hirtz (Seling 1839), a Protestant goldsmith, born 1667, master *c.*1689, died 1715.
The foot and lid embossed with cherubim-heads with outspread wings and scrolling acanthus in between. A beaded moulding separates the foot from the stem, the lower part of which is fluted with silver borders. The knop cast, with acanthus leaves and blank ovals. The openwork calyx of embossed, chased and fretted silver, again with putto-heads, acanthus leaves and affronted C-scrolls with grape clusters beneath.

*There is a silver-gilt ciborium of about 1690 (H. 32.5 cm) by this master in the Catholic parish church of St George, Trugenhofen (Kreis Heidenheim).*

115 Cruets and stand. (Cat. no.
22). Bolzano, *c.*1750. Maker's
mark *A.H.*

**22** *CRUETS AND STAND*
Silver-gilt.
L. of dish: 37 cm (14½ ins); h. of cruets: c. 16.5 cm (6½ ins).
Tyrolean. Town mark of Bolzano (R³7343) *c.*1750; maker's mark *AH*,
unidentified (R³7351).
Condition: regilt; the cruets repaired.
The dish embossed and chased with bold rocaille which balances, yet is
not symmetrical, and a wide variety of textures. There is a little joke on
the rim where there are rococo 'openings' embossed with 'waterfalls'
tumbling on to shells: one of the shells has a small frog on it. In between
are embossed scenes: Christ and the woman of Samaria, Tobias and the
Angel, the Finding of Moses, and a drayman walking by his cart
towards a stretch of water, with a church on the hill beyond, and a
miraculous image of the Virgin and Child in front of him.
The declivities in the centres of the dish are chased with *RV* in
monogram, and a coat of arms,
The cruets are ensuite.

*The arms are those of the Krauss von Sala unter Kraussegg family, whose seat*
*was at Castelruth in South Tyrol.[1] The cruets and stand must have been a*
*present from an unidentified member of the family, with the initials RV, to the*
*shrine depicted on the dish. This may be the Madonna Inviolata at Riva on*
*Lake Garda, then of course, part of the Habsburg empire. The story goes that in*
*1603 a drayman called Giovannino Brusaferro was leading his heavily loaded*
*cart when his little son fell off and was crushed by a wheel. The Virgin suddenly*
*appeared to him, his son was saved, and a sanctuary was built to commemorate the*
*event.[2].*

*There is a rococo holy-water bucket, embossed with the washing of the feet, by*
*the same goldsmith, in the North Bohemian Museum in Liberec, formerly*
*Reichenberg.[3] In the middle of the eighteenth century Bolzano was a still more*
*important goldsmithing centre than Innsbruck.*

NOTES
**1** J. Siebmacher, *Grosses und Allgemeines Wappenbuch,* Nürnberg, 1854-1901,vol. IV,
   pp. 9-10. I am most grateful to Mr Michael Holmes for identifying these arms.
**2** G Gumppenberg, G Maggia, and A. Zanella, *Atlante Mariano,* Verona, 1839-1847,
   vol.III, pp. 665-669.
**3** M. Rosenberg, *Der Goldschmiede Merkzeichen,* Bonn, 1928, vol. IV,
   p. 362.

**23** *CIBORIUM*

Silver-gilt.
H. 34 cm (13½ ins).
English. London mark for 1852-3; maker's mark of Charles Thomas Fox
and George Fox.
Condition: good.
The large, plain circular foot with cast acanthus leaves coming down on
to it from the acanthus stem. The knop a flattened sphere, and the bowl
and lid with unlobed acanthus-and-stamen cut-card work.

116 One each of two pairs of candlesticks. *Left* (Cat. no. 24): Utrecht, 1663, by Tymen van Leeuwen. *Right* (Cat. no. 25): Utrecht, 1698. Maker unidentified.

*Despite the neo-classicism of the individual decorative elements, this has a distinctly neo-Queen Anne appearance with its broad plain surface, and the cut-card work. Charles Thomas Fox (b. 1801) and George Fox (b. 1816) worked in partnership, producing some of the more distinguished and distinctive plate of the mid-nineteenth century. Some of their work was for the firm of Lambert & Rawlings, who also dealt in antique plate and who, no doubt, influenced the Foxes into making pieces in a variety of antique styles, from nine coasters in the manner of the 1770s to adaptations, hall-marked 1858, of the tazze of Summer and Winter in the auricular style, by Adam van Vianen, 1627.[1]*

NOTES
1 John Culme, *Nineteenth Century Silver*, London, 1977, pp. 76, 77, 217, 163, 167, 186.

**24** *PAIR OF ALTAR CANDLESTICKS*
Silver.
H. 41.3 cm (16¼ ins).
Dutch. Town mark of Utrecht; date letter *Z* for 1663; maker's mark of Tymen van Leeuwen, who registered his mark in 1652.[1] (cf. no. 33).
Condition: very worn and much repaired. The ball feet on one candlestick resoldered on, the flange above the knop broken.
On the base of each candlestick a plain oval cartouche, engraved: *Pitertie Dirkx Houdt niet Anno 1664*, and another: *P.D.H.N.*

*The inscription is obscure, but it may refer to a member of the Dierout family in whose house on the Nieuwe Graft in Utrecht, the hidden Catholic Church of St. Catherine was consecreated in 1664. The 1768 inventory of its contents includes an expositorium with silver mounts (no. 33?) four flower-pot fronts, (30 and 31?) and six smaller ones (32?), as well as perhaps these two candlesticks. Much of the silver vanished from the church, probably shortly after 1768, when the Jesuit incumbent was forced to leave.[2].*

*These are relatively early examples of the tripod baluster-stemmed altar-candlestick, the earliest ones of which appear in Holland in the 1630s.[3] The other design common during the mid-seventeenth century was the round-bottomed Salomonic or clustered column design.[4] The tripod form was to become standard for altar candlesticks from the late seventeenth century and throughout the eighteenth and nineteenth centuries.*

NOTES
1 *Merken der Utrechtse Edelsmieden 1598-1740*, Centraal Museum, Utrecht, no. 233.
2 The inventory is published in *Archief voor de geschiedenis van het Aartsbisdomb Utrecht* XLIII, 1917, pp. 64-67. I am very grateful to P. P. W. M. Dirkse, Rijksmuseum Het Catharijne Convent, Utrecht, for suggesting the provenance of these pieces.
3 J. W. Frederiks, *Dutch Silver*, vol. IV, The Hague, 1961, No. 105, of 1633 by Michiel de Bruyn of Utrecht.
4 *Op. cit.*, no. 111, of 1649, by the same maker.

117 One each of two pairs of candlesticks. *Left* (Cat. no. 27): Augsburg. 1700, by Johann Joachim I Lutz. Probably from Kreuzlingen, Switzerland. *Right* (Cat. no. 26): ditto with the arms of Melchior Lechner, Abbot of Kreuzlingen (1696-1707).

**25** *PAIR OF ALTAR CANDLESTICKS*
Silver-gilt.
H. (excluding the pricket): 68.4 cm (26½ ins).
Dutch. Town mark of Utrecht; date letter *M*, for 1698; maker's mark a comb-like device (unidentified).
Condition: the gilding original and very worn.
The tripod foot with putto heads crowning each volute. Swags of fruit embossed and chased on the edge of each, and a border of money-moulding down the sides. Each facet embossed with an oval cartouche beneath a shell, with acanthus leaves. The knop embossed with a swag of fruit and flowers and pounced with scrolls. The upper baluster stem encased with acanthus leaves and with three scrolling brackets which support the bell-shaped gadrooned drip pan.
For a possible provenance q.v. no. 24.

**26** *PAIR OF LARGE CANDLESTICKS*

Silver.
H. 77 cm (30¼ ins).
German. Town mark of Augsburg for 1700 (Seling 158); maker's mark of Johann Joachim I Lutz, (Seling 1827, cf. nos. 6 and 27).
Condition: one free-standing acanthus leaf broken off the baluster stem of one candlestick.
Embossed and chased. Large cast cherubim-heads with free-standing wings on the upper corners of the feet. Cherubim-heads and integral wings on the knop. Three oval cartouches on the feet, one engraved *IHS*; the second with the arms of Melchior I Lechner, abbot of Kreuzlingen (1696-1707) quartered with that of the abbey, the initials M A Z C (unidentified), and 1702; the third with the device of Kreuzlingen—a hand of God holding a cross and emerging from a cloud, and the inscription: *Capitulum Creux Linganum*.[1]

*Kreuzlingen, in the Canton of Thurgau, Switzerland, was formerly an Augustinian priory; it was secularised in 1848, and it was perhaps then that these candlesticks and cat. no. 27 were disposed of.[2] Pieces by Lutz, as well as by other Augsburg goldsmiths, remain in the treasury of the church.*

*Melchior Lechner, the son of a brewer, made his vows at the Priory of Kreuzlingen in 1678, but retained an involvement in political life, being* Statthalter *successively in Hirschlatt and Riedern. In 1696 he was elected prior, and although the priory's chronicler reproaches him for having conceded too much to the Bishop of Constance, his reputation lingers on in the many improvements which he made to the priory church, including the acquisition of these candlesticks.[3]*

NOTES
**1** J. Siebmacher, *Grosses und Allgemeines Wappenbuch,* Nürnberg, 1854-1901, vol. I, p. 52, pl. XXII. I am most grateful to Michael Holmes of the V & A for identifying the arms and device.
**2** A. Knoepfli, *Kunstführer durch die Schweiz,* Bern, 1971, pp. 660-662.

3  Q.v. the article on the abbots of Kreuzlingen by H. Lei, *Thurgauer Jahrbuch,* 1968, which includes an illustration of his portrait in the seminary. I am most grateful to H. U. Wepfer, of the Seminar Kreuzlingen, for sending me this information.

**27** *PAIR OF CANDLESTICKS*
Silver on an iron core.
H. 35.5 cm (13 ins).
German. Town mark of Augsburg for 1700 (Seling 158); maker's mark of Johann Joachim I Lutz (Seling 1827), cf. nos. 6 and 26.
Condition: good. The upper drip pans later additions.
The edge of the foot crimped, the foot itself embossed and chased with ragged and attenuated acanthus, and swags of very naturalistic flowers and fruit, against a matted ground. The spool-shaped bottom of the stem chased to resemble basket-work. The edge of the two gadrooned knops crimped. The long neck of the drip pan again as basket-work.

*If not necessarily ensuite with no. 26, these small candlesticks, by the same maker and of the same date, have many features in common with the large altar candlesticks from Kreuzlingen: the 'basket-work', the naturalism of the swags of fruit, the gadrooned elements with money-moulding between, and the cast moulding beneath the beading, so they may well have the same provenance.*

**28** *FOUR ALTAR CANDLESTICKS*
Silver-gilt.
H. 79 cm (29¼ ins).
Flemish. Town mark of Antwerp; date letter a crowned *M*, for 1738; maker's mark, a capital *S* (unidentified).
Condition: the gilding original and very worn.
Tripod scrolling feet with embossed putto-heads, sunflowers above and pendent husks below. Embossed eagles with free-standing wings on the volutes. The base of the stem with downward-pointing acanthus leaves. The baluster stem imbricated, with acanthus leaves wrapped over the surface. The vase-shaped element beneath the drip pan with a gadrooned lower section and triglyphs applied at intervals. The drip pan embossed with opposed S-scrolls, shells in between, and putto heads with swags of fruit connecting all together.

**29** *SIX ALTAR CANDLESTICKS*
Silver.
H. (excluding drip-pan and wooden base): 84 cm (33 ins).
Flemish. Town mark of Malines; the Imperial crown over *80*, for 1780 maker's mark, an anchor (unidentified).
Condition: poor; due to the thinness of the metal; there are many cracks, mostly repaired with solder. The drip-pans modern.
The candlesticks rise from a tripod base, embossed with long attenuated

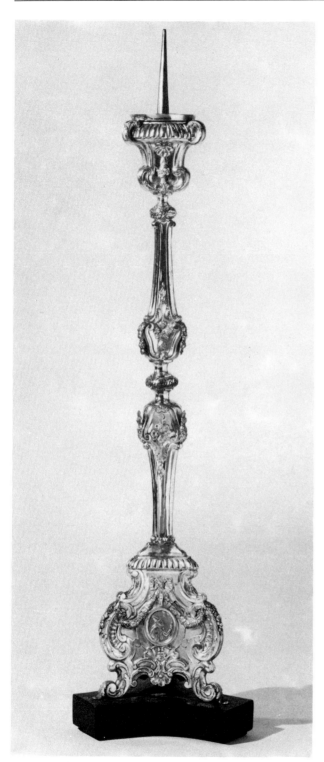

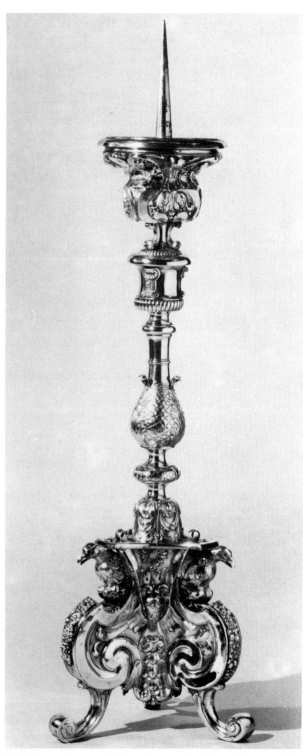

118 One of a set of four candlesticks. (Cat. no. 28). Antwerp, 1738. Maker unidentified.

119 One of a set of six altar candlesticks. (Cat. no. 29). Malines, *c.*1780. Maker unidentified.

scrolls, which form the main outlines. The knops are embossed and chased with guilloche ornament enclosing rosettes, a sign of encroaching neo-classicism. As a whole, however, despite its late date, the design remains rococo in its slender proportions and in the naturalism of the flower garlands above and below the knop and the raffled acanthus frills. The oval cartouches on the base are embossed with the Virgin, St Joseph and St Augustine (?—a bishop holding a flaming heart to heaven).

120 Altar-vase fronts. (Cat. nos. 32 (*left*) and 30 (*right*). Utrecht, 1715 (*left*) and 1718 (*right*), by Nicolaes Verhaer.

**30** *PAIR OF LARGE VASES*
Silver-gilt with silver decoration.
H. 23.5 cm (9¹/₁₀ ins).
Dutch. Town mark of Utrecht; date letter *G* for 1718; maker's mark of Nicolaes Verhaer, a Catholic goldsmith, born before 1687, son of the painter Arnoldus Verhaer and Cornelia van der Sloot; master in 1710, died 1750.[1]
Condition: dented and worn. The gilding original.
The foot gadrooned, the calyx of alternating acanthus and lotus leaves. The central coat of arms with a lion rampant holding a sickle moon and star in right paw (unidentified). Separate swags of fruit and foliage hanging from the S-scroll handles.
For a possible provenance q.v. no. 24.

*These are for decorating the altar, and as they are only seen from afar, the maker has economised on the silver by making merely a dummy, which stands in front of the true container. Verhaer was a popular goldsmith, much of whose surviving work was for the Catholic church, which, although officially prohibited in the Netherlands from 1581 onwards, in fact flourished in homes and secret churches. Pieces by him in the Centraal Museum in Utrecht include a statue of St Joseph holding the infant Jesus (1715-16); four large altar candlesticks (1724); a ciborium (1722?); a crown for a statue of the Virgin (1734); and a pepperpot (1740).[2]*

NOTES
**1** *Zilver Collectie Centraal Museum Utrecht,* catalogue, Utrecht, 1972, p. 72.
**2** *Op. cit.,* ills. 62, 66, 67, 74, 79: inv. nos. 11363; 15254 t/m; 15259; 16637; 17628.

**31** *PAIR OF LARGE VASES (ensuite with no. 30)*

Silver-gilt with silver decoration.
H. 22.5 cm (8¾ ins).
Dutch; about 1718; presumably Utrecht, but all marks illegible.
By another hand from that of no. 30.
For a possible provenance q.v. no. 24.

**32** *SIX SMALL VASE FRONTS (ensuite with no.30)*

Silver-gilt with silver decoration.
H. 13.2 cm (5¹/₁₀ ins).
Dutch. Town mark of Utrecht (twice); four vases with the date letter *D,* for 1715, and two with *E,* for 1716; maker's mark of Nicolaes Verhaer (cf. no. 30).
Condition: dented and worn. The gilding original.
The form is that of a wine cooler, with a gadrooned foot and calyx. A shield in the centre, on an imbricated cartouche, engraved *IHS.* The scroll handles beaded, and swags of fruit and foliage around the edge.
For a possible provenance q.v. no. 24.

**33** *SURROUND FOR A MONSTRANCE*

The columns and cresting silver-gilt, the scrolls and putti, silver, parcel-gilt.
H. (excluding plinth): 120 cm (3 ft 11¼ ins).
Dutch. Town mark of Utrecht and date letter *B*, for 1665; on the base of the columns, the Pelican in Piety and the Dove; maker's mark of Tymen van Leeuwen (cf. no. 24); town mark of Utrecht twice over on the side scrolls and flying putti; date letter *C*, for 1714; maker's mark of Nicolaes Verhaer (cf. no. 30).
Condition: the gilding original and very worn.
The whole is made of embossed and chased silver sheet with iron supports at the back, apart from the Salomonic columns and their bases, which are hollow but three-dimensional.

*The construction would have been erected on an altar to celebrate special liturgical occasions, framing the monstrance at the Exposition of the Blessed Sacrament. The iconography is appropriate to this: the Pelican in Piety, a traditional symbol of Christ and the Passion, and above, the dove of the Holy Ghost, the third person of the Trinity. It is used nowadays to surround the reliquary bust of St Philip Neri (no. 34), when this is displayed on his feast-day.*

*Although fifty years separate the two parts of this triumphal arch, there is no doubt that they belong together, as the side scrolls and putti form a compositional unity with the earlier section.*

*For a contemporary expositorium, as such things are called, compare the one made by N. Kalf in Cologne in 1678 for the Cathedral of Munster, Westphalia, This consists of a tall ebony base covered with embossed flowers, and with Salomonic columns, an arch of flowers, surmounted by an Imperial crown over the Dove, and two large floating putti holding candlesticks.[1]*

NOTE
1 *Rheinische Goldschmiedekunst der Renaissance und Barockzeit*, exhibition, Rheinisches Landesmuseum, Bonn, 1975, cat. no. 26, ill. 69.

**34** *RELIQUARY BUST OF ST PHILIP NERI*

Silver, with copper-gilt decoration and copper-gilt base, subsequently set with a diamond and emerald ring.
H. (excluding halo): 36 cm (14¼ ins).
Italian. Town mark of Rome (Bulgari 144?),[1] *c.*1810; maker's mark, a downward-pointing lance (?) (unidentified). Also stamped with a tax-exemption mark in use 1812-1815 (Bulgari 159), and with the .800 standard mark for second-hand items put on to the market again (Bulgari 164).
Condition: good.
The head cast, the shoulders of wrought plate, with chased decoration which is the only individual contribution by the goldsmith.

*The bust is an example of competent 'mass-produced' devotional art. The saint is shown in ecstasy, dressed as a priest ready to say mass, in alb, amice, and*

*Opposite page:*
121 Surround, originally for a monstrance. (Cat. no. 33). Utrecht. The columns, arch and Dove, 1665, by Tymen van Leeuwen; the sidescrolls and putti, 1714, by Nicolaes Verhaer. *Beneath* (Cat. no. 34), a reliquary bust of St Philip Neri. Roman, *c.*1810.

122 Angel Reliquary. (Cat. no. 35). Silver and copper-gilt. Italian. Circle of Alessander Algardi: mid seventeenth century.

*chasuble. This representation derives from the most celebrated sculptural depiction of the saint, the marble statue commissioned by Pietro Buoncompagni and executed by Alessandro Algardi between 1635 and 1638 for the sacristy of the Chiesa Nuova in Rome, the mother-house of the Oratorians.[2] This, rather than the straight-forward portrait bust modelled by Algardi on a death-mask of the saint (of which the prime original, dated 1640, is a bronze bust now in the Museum of the Rhode Island School of Design, and of which the Oratory possesses a later cast dated 1673), is by far the commonest source for busts of St Philip Neri.*

NOTES
1  C. Bulgari, *Argentieri, Gemmari e Orafi d'Italia*, Rome, 1958, vol. I, pp. 30-32.
2  Cf. Jennifer Montagu 'Alessandro Algardi and the statue of St Philip Neri; *Jahrbuch der Hamburger Kunstsammlungen* 22 (1977), pp. 75-100. I am most grateful to Alastair Laing for this reference.

## 35 *ANGEL RELIQUARY*

The angel and cartouche of silver; the wings, reliquary casket, cloud and base of copper-gilt.
H. 27.5 cm (10¹³⁄₁₆ ins); h. of angel without cloud, 16 cm (6¼ ins).
Italian. Mid-17th century.
The statuette and base cast. The wings, cloud and cartouche wrought, the last embossed with a flaming heart. The casket containing a relic of St Philip Neri.

*This reliquary is derived from the angel supporting the book for St Philip Neri (cf. no. 34) in the sculptural group by Algardi in the sacristy of the Chiesa Nuova in Rome (1635-38). This inspired a number of derivations, not only on a similar monumental scale in marble, and in the form of busts, but also on a reduced scale in silver.[1] The most similar of these last to the present statuette (differences being in the position of the arms and the shape of the wings) is the left-hand angel of the pair supporting the reliquary of St Feliciano in the Treasury of S Lorenzo in Florence.[2]*

*Such a cast statuette could have been made at any point in the second half of the seventeenth or early eighteenth century, and the dating of this one is based upon the style of the cartouche with its traces of the auricular in the upper part.*

NOTES
1  Cf. Jennifer Montagu, 'Alessandro Algardi and the statue of St Philip Neri', *Jahrbuch der Hamburger Kunstsammlungen* 22 (1977), pp. 75-100. I am most grateful to Alastair Laing for this reference and for pointing out this connection.
2  I am most grateful to Dr Jennifer Montagu for this information, which is to be included in her forthcoming book on Algardi.

123 Monstrance. (Cat. no. 36). London 1849 by R & S Garrard.

124 Monstrance. (Cat. no. 38). Belgian or German? mid nineteenth century; the circle of putto heads and clouds late seventeenth or eighteenth century.

**36** *MONSTRANCE*

Silver-gilt, set with cabochon garnets and facetted topazes (?).
H. 45.5 cm (17⅞ ins).
English. London date letter for 1849-50; maker's mark of Robert
Garrard, and stamped: *R & S GARRARD PANTON ST LONDON.*
Condition: good. The gilding original.
The foot shaped as a trefoil with rectangular projections in between the
foils. The upper surfaces swelling to form lobes while those of the projections are covered with applied acanthus leaves and end in classical
shells; from one of the leaves rises a cast branch, growing both vines and
corn husks, which trails asymmetrically around the foot. The lower
stem hexagonal and stepped, the upper stem swelling and then tapering
upwards with rococo foliage wrapping over the swelling and with Gothic
lobes at the top. The vine and corn branch continues to wind its way up
the stem. The reverse of the join between star-burst and stem covered
with a free-standing cast palm-branch. The finial a cross moline.

*R. & S. Garrard & Co., were, together with Hunt & Roskell and C. F.
Hancock's, the most important London silversmiths of the second third of the
nineteenth century. Their silver is nearly always well-modelled and finely
chased; this monstrance has both these qualities. Its design is eclectic, with Gothic
lobing on the foot and stem, classical scrolls and shells also on the foot, a rococo
knop, a naturalistic vine and a palm branch at the back, cast no doubt from the
same model as ones on the table centrepieces for which Garrards were renowned.*

*It must be one of the earliest monstrances to have been made in this country
during the Catholic revival (the restoration of the hierarchy was not until 1850)
and this may partly explain its rather uncertain design. It is likely that it was
obtained for the first London Oratory in King William Street.*

**37** *MONSTRANCE*

Silver-gilt, with silver decoration and set with jewellery.
H. 107 cm (3 ft 6 ins).
French. Mid-nineteenth century. Stamped with a French export mark in
use between 1840 and 1879, and an unidentified marker's mark: *CT* in a
lozenge with a pitcher in between.
Condition: the stem and upper part regilt.
The base in the heavy late neo-classical style, with silver cherubs. The
urn-shaped knop and stem embossed with angel heads and acanthus,
with swags of naturalistic grapes over them. Beneath the sunburst are
grapes and wheatsheaves. The whole decorated with items of jewellery.
On the base: a diamond and opal sickle-moon brooch, a heart-shaped
opal pendant surrounded by diamonds and pink topaz, hanging from a
true-lovers's knot set with diamonds and opals; an oval opal brooch set
about with pearls, single opals, an opal bar brooch and an oval opal
surrounded by pearls on the reverse: all late nineteenth century in date.
Early twentieth century ruby and diamond rosettes also on the reverse.
On the stem, a solitaire rose-cut diamond. On the cluster of grapes a

diamond pendant/brooch of about 1860; above, part of a pink topaz and pearl hair ornament; below the *lunula* a pavé-set diamond heart and sickle-moon, and the *lunula* itself outlined by diamonds and cabochon garnets; more of the half ornaments over the *lunula* and a necklace *ensuite* around the rays; the Greek cross finial also en suite.

### 38 *MONSTRANCE*

The foot and stem copper-gilt, the rest silver-gilt, set with a cross of seven diamonds beneath the finial cross with its amethysts (foiled pink topazes?) and pearls; the *lunula* diamond-studded, and ten cabochon garnets around the centre.
Possibly Belgian or German, mid-nineteenth century; the circle of putto heads and the corresponding circle of clouds behind, late seventeenth or eighteenth century. The garnets probably a late-nineteenth century addition.
H. 81 cm (32 ins).

*The style of the baluster stem, with its putto heads and acanthus leaves, and the embossed acanthus leaves on the foot are all in imitation of features of late-seventeenth century baroque design. The hand which embosssed the putto heads and clouds in the upper part is clearly not that which executed the foot and stem, and is much freer and more spontaneous. Similar rings of putti appear on baroque monstrances made in Germany, and in Belgium.[1] The craftsman must have had some parts of an older monstrance and devised this design around them. The finial cross is in the late neo-classical style current until the middle of the nineteenth century; cabochon-cut stones, however, only became popular in the last third of the nineteenth century, so they are almost certainly later additions.*

*NOTE*
**1** P. Colman, *L'Orfèvrerie religieuse Liègeoise*, Liège, 1966, II, ills. 147 (1702/3), 150 (1776), and 151 (1780).

### 39 *RING SET WITH A NUGGET OF GOLD*

Mean diam. of ring 2.9 cm (1³/₁₆ ins).
About 1852-3.
The hoop plain in the lower half, the upper half pentagonal and engraved, on one shoulder: *Rev. Adm. Doctori J. H. Newman* (To the Reverend and Admirable Doctor J. H. Newman); and on the other: *Vero Fidei Defensori. Cath. California* (a true defender of the Faith, from the Catholics of California).

*In 1851 John Newman delivered a detailed account, to an audience in the Corn Exchange, Birmingham, of the offences committed by the ex-Dominican, Achilli, who for some time had been touring England to great acclaim, sponsored by the violently anti-Catholic Protestant Alliance. Newman's aim was not only to unmask a hypocrite, who had been found guilty by the Inquisition in Rome of seducing very young women but to silence a voice which had been putting out a great deal of inflammatory and untrue anti-Catholic propaganda, which was all the more eagerly received in England for being salacious and sensational.*

*The Protestant Alliance responded by charging Newman with libel, and from that moment until 1853 the threat of prison hung over his head. Despite the testimony of two of Achilli's victims, specially brought back from Italy, the trial, which was heard in June 1852, was conducted with such anti-Catholic bias that Newman was found guilty. By this time his costs were enormous, his solicitor's bill alone amounting to £2,300, so an international indemnity fund was set up. Money flooded in from Europe and America, this nugget of gold being a most touchingly down-to-earth contribution from gold-rush California. Eventually it amounted to £2,000 more than was needed, and the surplus went towards the building of Newman's University Church in Dublin.*

*In January 1853, Newman was sentenced, but by this time respectable opinion, including* The Times, *agreed that his trial had been unfair and his sentence was a relatively light £100 fine. It was the climax of the first half of his public life, and English Catholics henceforth saw him as their champion, although he was in disgrace with society for some years for having had the indelicacy to raise such matters.[1]*

NOTE

**1** M. Trevor, *Newman, The Pillar of the Cloud*, London, 1962, pp. 554-632.

125 Ring set with a nugget of gold. (Cat. no. 39). Presented to John Henry Newman by the Catholics of California. *c.*1852-3.

# THE ORATORY MUSICAL TRADITION

## *Henry Washington*

'You mean: *sing it as though you were DEAD!*'
From the back row of the choir Old Spencer's voice broke the respectful silence of the practice-room. Not quite the clarion call he had intended to sound; more of a hiss, in fact. Yet richly evocative as hisses go. In a single breath it effused the disparate emotions of bitterness, disillusion and contempt!

This was the London Oratory Choir at rehearsal circa 1935. We had been studying the Gregorian Proper of the Mass according to the 'new-fangled' rhythmic theory put forward—long before, nevertheless—by the learned Benedictine monks of Solesmes. This idea of a 'free musical rhythm' was the outcome of many years of paleographic research into mediaeval manuscripts enshrined in the archives of certain European religious houses.

My devotion to these Benedictine Scholastics was boundless and unremitting. I had made a study of their monumental *Paleographie Musicale*, with its facsimiles and revealing analyses of the ancient melodies, rejoicing in the universal acclaim that crowned their patient investigations. Guéranger, Pothier, Mocquéreau, Gajard, Desroquettes; these revered names, with their own peculiar euphony, seemed to me worthy of a place in some future litany. Heaven forbid that any further studies should disclose the 'truth' of a *metrical* interpretation of the manuscripts; for no alternative solution could ever outweigh the spiritual efficacy and sheer musical beauty of the Solesmes restorations. Shall we ever know for sure that Divine intervention was not at hand to compensate for the vexing obscurities of mediaeval cryptology?

These were troublous times ...It was on the wave of liturgical reform first promulgated by Pope Pius X in his *Motu Proprio* (1903) and later underlined by Pius XI in his *Divini Cultus* (1928), that the Fathers of the London Oratory appointed me to the post of Musical Director, as best-equipped lay exponent of the reformed Chant, in addition to my well-established interpretative knowledge of sixteenth-century polyphony.

I took up my Oratory duties on Passion Sunday, 1935, confronted with the onerous task of preparing music for the Offices of Palm Sunday, Holy Week and Easter. Earlier that year Fr Clement Bevan (1890-1958), my first Prefect of Music, had attended High Mass at St Chad's Cathedral, Birmingham, where I was Organist and Choirmaster. He came stealthily and unannounced and accompanied by James Long, the brother of Kathleen Long, the distinguished pianist and renowned interpreter of Mozart. They represented a *concorso* of Oratory Fathers, supported by certain musical advisers who had already considered many applications for the posts of Musical Director and Organist. They listened to my Solesmes Chant, Palestrina Mass and Victoria motet; and to my organ-playing of Bach and Rheinberger. I was engaged on the spot as Organist, with the prospect of assuming complete responsibility for the musical administration. Soon after, I was elected to the position of Musical Director on the additional recommendation of—among others—Dom Bernard McElligott OSB (Founder of the Society of St Gregory); the Principal and tutors of the Birmingham and Midland Institute School of Music, including Dr Allen K. Blackall, under whom I had studied composition; and G. D. Cunningham, City Organist, who during a course of study taught me—by example—how to *teach* organ-playing!.

As to the composition of the choir and its condition, I found that, whilst the boy choristers were more than competent, the adult members were not above criticism. 'Old Spencer', quoted above, was but one of a handful of ageing professionals, drawn largely from theatre and concert platforms, who were at pains to impresss the 'new guvnor' with fervently-warbled vestiges of what had been—beyond question—a long and glorious musical past.

Joe Boddy was tenor soloist, and well past his prime; Teddy Shale, who had once been tenor soloist, was now engaged in the important job of Choir Librarian and Accountant. He had been for many years stage manager at the Theatre Royal, Drury Lane. Charlie Carr and Leslie Dawson were the other tenors. There were four altos: Oliver, Madden, Bradford (an amateur composer of merit), and—the salvation of the line —a young man called Johnnie Maggs. On the bass line were Tommie Rainger (a friend of Barclay, the retired Musical Director), Iago Lewis (a heavy baritone with a very slow *vibrato*), Griffiths (*basso profundo*) and a younger man named Robinson with a powerful voice—a bit *too* power-ful—but he more than compensated for the waning powers of his bench-mates. 'Old Spencer' completed the set! When Lewis once absent-mindedly usurped his stand Spencer cut him dead for months to follow!

Before long I engaged four new singers, who were destined to give valuable service for many years to come: Charlie Whitehead (alto), man-ager of the wine department in the Civil Service Stores in the Strand; Arthur Scott (bass), solicitor; Frank Murray (tenor) and Sid Carr (light baritone), both teachers at the Oratory Central School. By a strange coincidence Frank and Sid each had two brothers who were called to the priesthood; Dom Gregory and Joe Murray, and Charles and Tony Carr.

But to return to the choir before the advent of those Four Just Men. The Chant was being sung from Ratisbon and Mechlin choir books. It was often 'recited' on a monotone in manner invariably heroic, challeng-ing and assertive, regardless of the spiritual content of the Latin text. Now they were going to have to learn to 'pray' the Chant in flowing musical periods; though as yet, to these old stagers, the terms *Ictus, Episema* and *Arsis* and *Thesis* were only so many dirty words! An eminent Catholic choirmaster, Donald Edeson, Secretary of the Society of St Gregory and Editor of *Music and Liturgy*, wrote to me with the advice: 'Chuck out those old-timers and start afresh with new blood.'

153

126 Henry Washington. A photograph taken about 1950.

127 Fr Clement Bevan as a young priest.

He had done just that with outstanding success in his own North London parish, St Joseph's Retreat, Highgate; but I was not then disposed to adopt so sweeping a course. Some five years earlier I had been faced with the same daunting prospect of training an ageing choir at St Chad's Cathedral, Birmingham. I there found myself endowed with an unfashionable virtue called Compassion. Instead of 'chucking them out', I elected to win them over. Resentment soon gave way to understanding and respect—even affection. Now at the Oratory, 'Old Spencer', who was an art dealer of note, took me to his gallery on Paddington Green and proudly displayed his fine collection. Tommie Rainger, whom I reluctantly suspended for insolence, returned after a short repentant absence. Griffiths sought my company as sympathetic adviser on his personal problems, and dear old Bradford gave me the key to his thatched country cottage in Oxfordshire.

On my appointment, Fr Bevan pointed out that previous Oratory musicians had all been long-lived, and that I was only the third in line as Musical Director. My immediate predecessor, Arthur Barclay, had taken over at the early age of twenty-four on the death (in 1893) of his tutor, the distinguished Thomas Wingham, who had been musical Director since two years before the Opening and Dedication of the present church

in 1884. For close on half a century, Barclay with his organist friend and colleague Edward D'Evry, enjoyed the admiration of a wide circle of music-lovers who, on Sundays and Feast Days, would crowd the side-chapels facing the Choir Gallery; a veritable 'audience', listening to superb concert performances—sometimes with orchestra—of Latin masterpieces by the great classical composers of the eighteenth century. Nevertheless, the exalted polyphonists of the Renaissance such as Palestrina and Victoria held a restricted place in the repertoire. Even the Masses of our own William Byrd were included …but only during the 'Penitential' seasons of Lent and Advent!

On my first Easter Sunday I was directed to produce Palestrina's glorious *Missa Papae Marcelli*. The performance at that short notice could not have foreshadowed later triumphs in Palestrina style; but in that hour I was blissfully ignorant of the appalling impact the choice of programme must have had upon an 'audience' anticipating a soul-stirring execution of, say, Beethoven's Mass in D or Mozart's 'Coronation'.

Barclay had lately resigned in a huff—taking his music with him—at the gentle suggestion that in his declining years he might train a younger man to become his worthy successor. Arthur Barclay *Jones*—to give him his full name—rejoiced in the title of 'Musical Director'; which might have become my own description had I not observed that it sounded to

128 Choir group taken in the Oratory garden in 1908. Fr Ralph Kerr is the Prefect of Music. On his right is Arthur Barclay; on his left is Iago Lewis with Thomas Rainger beyond. Behind Fr Kerr and Barclay stands A.J. Spencer. *(London Oratory album)*.

129 Choir group taken in the Oratory garden in 1911. Fr Wilfrid Burnham is the Prefect of Music. On his right is Edward D'Evry; on his left Arthur Barclay. Behind them, from left to right, stand Iago Lewis, Charles Carr, and A.J. Spencer. Seated in the front row, from left to right, are Teddy Shale, Sinclair Mantell, and Thomas Rainger. *(London Oratory album).*

me like a Director who happened to be fond of music. Yet the Fathers raised no objection to my being styled 'Director of Music' instead. After all, the conductor of every theatre orchestra in the land was invariably called Musical Director as he is to this day. He would have been a well-trained musician who supplemented a possibly meagre income by the 'drudgery' of teaching.

Many musical directors achieved renown outside their theatrical commitments; to mention but one, the famous Edward German, whose operas and orchestral suites atttained great and lasting popularity. Incidentally, *his* full name was Edward German *Jones*. Arthur Barclay Jones of the Oratory was no less distinguished both as composer and conductor. I saw a privately-owned copy of his motet *Postula a me* which he wrote for the lately-instituted Feast of Christ the King. It included a fine bass solo which, by all accounts, used to be most impressively delivered by his friend, Thomas Rainger, *soi-disant* 'basso-cantante', soloist, Brompton Oratory!

Although I never met Barclay I had once seen him 'in action', at the Oratory (he appeared to be using a wand with a knob at the tip!). One could not but comply—if regretfully—with his wish that his compositions should no longer be available after his departure. I should have welcomed a meeting; but in all the circumstances the Fathers felt that no good purpose could be served by my seeking his acquaintance.

Edward D'Evry had also retired—he was in his mid-seventies—but he graciously offered to stay on to see me through my first few weeks. He was a man of considerable personal charm. He promptly took me under his wing; showing me the ropes, tendering fatherly advice, and wining and dining me at his favourite hotel. His extempore organ-playing was an enchantment; as a Postlude to Mass or Vespers he would often improvise at length on salient Gregorian *motifs* of the Feast. A sometime Prefect of Music, Fr Wilfrid Burnham (1861-1938)—short, erect, impassive—once asked D'Evry the title of the piece he had played after Vespers. D'Evry gratified at the interest thus shown, replied expansively: 'Vierne, dear Father, Louis Vierne of Notre Dame. A *Symphonie* —Organ Symphony, you know. Very fine, very fine!' Fr Burnham, stiffly: '*I didn't like it!*'

Biographical information about D'Evry is limited. He was a Fellow of the Royal College of Organists, and of Trinity College, London. He was not included in Grove's *Dictionary of Music and Musicians*, though the post-war edition of *Who's Who in Music* connects him with Trinity College of Music and the Brompton Oratory, giving specific dates. His compositions for organ (published by Novello) were pleasingly melodious; and his setting of the Magnificat was by far the best of the few 'figured' examples of that canticle sung at the Oratory. I believe he was a pupil of Vincent D'Indy, who after 1873 became the most prominent of César Franck's disciples. Arthur Barclay—also missing from Grove—is no more fully documented, though an 'Appreciation' of the Oratory's music, dated 1902, gives us the following vignette. 'This refined and reverent singing and the general efficiency of the choir is due to its excellent trainer, Mr Arthur Barclay, L.R.A.M. This gentleman was a chorister at the Oratory and received his musical education at the Guidhall School of Music, where he is now a professor and teacher of harmony, piano and orchestration. Mr Barclay is not only an accomplished musician, but a born choir-trainer. He has the rare capacity for not only teaching boys correct vocalisation, but for training them to sing in a refined, artistic manner, the result of which is that his choristers have a beautiful purity of tone. All praise is due to him for the efficient way in which his choir renders the fine music. There are few places where the dignified music of the sixteenth century can be heard so well sung as at Brompton.'

Within twelve months of my own appointment, Ralph Downes arrived to fill to perfection the role of Organist; the happy culmination of an exhaustive and, at times, invidious search for the most suitable candidate. As a leading musician of wide acclaim, Ralph's skill and good taste at the console was equalled only by an enviable modesty and deference of demeanour. He relinquished a valuable post at Princeton University to return to his native land, and he and I soon forged a bond of co-operation and friendship that has survived to this day. Before his coming it fell to my lot to supply the heavy demand for organ-playing at the daily Night Services (sic), and at weddings, etc. Downes made a comprehensive study of the baroque organ, and duly redesigned the London Oratory instrument on classical lines—an enterprise long overdue. He was responsible for the fine organ in the Festival Hall on the South Bank, and has ever since been in demand as consultant in the specification of new organs and re-builds throughout the United Kingdom and abroad.

In sixteenth century Rome, St Philip Neri always employed the name 'Oratory', for his meetings of instruction in the Christian philosophy of life, wherever they might be held. This may be regarded as an extension of the oft-quoted injunction: 'Domus mea domus orationis vocabitur, dicit Dominus'. It would seem therefore that an Oratory is both a *place* —a house or simply a room—as well as an *occasion* for prayer and preaching. But more than that; for St Philip, himself a lover of music, attached great importance to the singing of psalms, hymns and spiritual canticles as a medium for raising the heart and mind to Almighty God. Ever since that time the Saint's disciples, known as the Congregation of the Oratory, have cherished the idea of music as a precious adjunct to the celebration of the Mass and Office, and any other subsidiary devotions. The illustrious Palestrina was a friend of the 'Apostle of Rome', who, it is claimed, became his Father Confessor. He attended the religious exercises; and, like Animuccia, composed many *Laudi Spirituali* expressly to adorn those pious reunions. Thus came about the term *Oratorio* to describe, in later times, any large-scale work based for the most part on a religious text; though there is no reason to suppose that the congregation of the Oratory had any part in its development. Occasional performances of appropriate works of this nature have been customary for many years past at Brompton and Birmingham. Among them may be mentioned the Verdi and Mozart *Requiems*. Elgar's *The Dream of Gerontius*, Monteverdi's *Vespers*, and the Palestrina, Rossini and Dvorak settings of the *Stabat Mater*. Mendelssohn's *Lauda Sion* is bound up with *Quarant' Ore* (the Forty Hours devotion to the Blessed Sacrament), and the Good Friday evening devotion *Maria Desolata* would be not quite the same without Dvorak's beautiful *Stabat Mater*. In the 'bad old days'—1899 to be exact—the observance of Good Friday included a performance of Tchaikowsky's *Pathétique* Symphony! On the Good Friday of 1936 I believe I persuaded Fr Juvenal Matthews (1901-1970)— then Prefect of Music—to sanction a complete performance of Dvorak's *Stabat Mater* instead of the three 4-part excerpts that had served to represent the work by tradition. The programme slips included the whole sequence printed in Latin with a side-by-side English translation. At the end of the first movement—which must have taken between fifteen and twenty minutes—a distraught Fr Juvenal was at my elbow almost tearfully imploring me to cut it down to make room for the three Discourses that were usually interpolated: The complete masterpiece—so painstakingly prepared—was never to be heard at Brompton...

The ceremonies of Passiontide and Easter are the most important and the oldest in the liturgical calendar. This holy season fostered from its very beginning some of the greatest and most inspiring music of all time. How one must deplore the recent omission of that lovely Gospel Tone, surely of Jewish origin and perhaps the oldest form of chant to have survived. At the Oratory, in addition to the full presentation of the ancient melodies, we included all eighteen of the Victoria responsories for the second and third Nocturns of Tenebrae. Tomas Louis de Victoria, though a priest—which his exact contemporary Palestrina never became —reflected in his music a more emotional amd dramatic approach to the text; never more fully revealed than in these moving responsories.I was deepy affected by this human expressiveness and elicited it from my singers with increasing intensity as the years went by. Tenebrae closed after Allegri's impressive *Miserere*, the score of which had always been jealously hidden at St Peter's. It was not revealed until the youthful Mozart heard it sung there and promptly transcribed it from memory. Space here precludes an exhaustive list of the powerful polyphonic settings specific to Holy Week at the Oratory. They have come down through the years with little revision, though I introduced Jacob Handl's *Benedictus* canticle and Byrd's *St John Passion*; and Fr Patrick Bushell produced a most acceptable version of the *Crux Fidelis* attributed to King John of Portugal. Since then, I believe the Holy Week programme has remained unaltered.

With the rapid development of the choir's liturgico-musical standards came a gradual modification of the Community's directives. It appeared that a few of the older—perhaps less enlightened—Fathers feared a growing neglect of the earlier operatic style concerts. Fr Kenneth Dale-Roberts (1882-1972) was the prime example of the *Laudator temporis acti*, though he never once disclosed his disapproval of the new regime. Indeed, such was the effect of his unfailing charm of manner that years passed before I realised that he could never in this life be reconciled to the heavenly quality of such music as would have charmed the ear and lifted the heart of our holy father St Philip himself. Not that insofar as the classics were retained they suffered any degree of musical restraint. This was a matter both Downes and I had qualms about for a short period. In 1904—the year I was born—it is on record that Barclay performed the *Kyrie* of Haydn's First Mass in so subdued a manner and excessively slow tempo that the character of the composition was entirely transformed. This expedient, though resorted to from the highest motives—was to my mind nothing short of musical vandalism; somehow comparable by inversion to the present-day cult of 'jazzing up' the more appealing melodies of Chopin or Schubert. Papa Haydn must have turned in his grave; for had he not boasted that he could write the psalm *Miserere* in *tempo allegro?* Such was the natural joyousness of his spirit.

But I for one was beginning to have a liking to these Viennese *chefs-d'oeuvres* I had previously despised as unworthy of liturgical inclusion. Far from tempering the wind to the shorn lamb, I quickly concluded that whatever music was put before me must be brought to perfection of performance in its proper style; for the music's sake, regardless of time and place. In the Oratory church I certainly reacted impressionably to the beautiful Italian Renaissance architecture after the dim religious light of Pugin's German Gothic at St Chad's Cathedral. And so I persevered *con amore* to achieve musical perfection in its own right from the masterpieces of my new idols, Mozart, Haydn, Beethoven and the others, with no less fervour than I had always bestowed on my adored masters of the Renaissance. I admit to an immense enjoyment of these Viennese frolics—as music-making—but during Holy Mass, not without scruples! I still feel disconcerted by 'Haydn in church'. Rome has consistently condemned music of a secular nature as an adjunct to the performance of the Sacred Mysteries. The classical composers as often as not produced church music to gratify the taste of their princely patrons. There is a place for musical frivolity, but that place is not the House of Prayer—certainly not during an act of Divine Worship! ...Suffer an old-fashioned opinion to go on record.

May I say here that I regard the Oratory musical tradition to be worthily upheld at the present time in the capable hands of John Hoban and Patrick Russill. Perhaps John Hoban will assent to my view that his own musical horizon has similarly widened in the Oratory's ambience, since he first made his mark with the *Scuola di Chiesa* by an exclusive devotion to music of the Polyphonic Schools?

Weddings and requiems, as ever, came in abundance. These were graded musically and ceremonially according to taste and expense. Requiems were either plainsong; small choir (Casciolini); or full choir (Victoria). Organ weddings, shared at mutual convenience between

130 Choir group taken in the Little Oratory in 1977. From left to right:
Back row: Christopher Robson, Cyril Ellis, Edgar Fleet, Richard Bourne, George Dingsdace, Richard Stuart.
Middle row: John Hoban (Director), Joyce Jarvis, John Dudley, Ann Blake, Christopher Rice, Richard Codd, Patrick Russill (Organist).
Front row: Nancy Long, Rachel Bevan, Margaret Archibald, Petronella Dittmer, Mavis Beattie, Ruth Lindley.

Organist and Musical Director; small choir weddings when the Musical Director both played the organ and directed the choir; and full choir weddings involving both Musical Director and Organist. On these latter occasions large sums of money must have been expended on floral decorations and the laying of an endless red carpet the full length of the aisle. Clark, the Head Verger, was a tower of strength to all concerned at these ceremonies. Slim and elegant in his spendid green livery, he delicately addressed the bride as *Miss* until the nuptials were completed, when he was careful to call her *Madam*. He had previously been in private service. If the priest who was 'taking' the wedding ran into trouble with the parties insisting on the playing of 'The' *Ave Maria* (Bach-Gounod), *The Mountains of Mourne,* or *The Arrival of the Queen of Sheba*, he would refer them to Mr Washington, who, they were assured, would prove 'a hard nut to crack'. This was where diplomacy prevailed and, with no bones broken, I always won the day. However, it was no decision of my own that once prevented the renowned Count John McCormack singing *Panis Angelicus*, or whatever else, when he turned up at a wedding with a sheaf of music under his arm. The sight of that legendary figure seated disconsolately among the wedding guests was almost heart-rending. 'I took my harp to a party and nobody asked me to play...' As to the *Ave Maria*, one can but admire Gounod's ingenious superscription of a graceful melody to the *C major Prelude* of Bach. But at the period in question the Fathers steadfastly forbade its use as being too hackneyed—as was Handel's 'celebrated' *Largo*—though the prohibition of such items was later to be rescinded. On the other hand, exception was never taken to the use of organ arrangements of Wagner's *Bridal Chorus* from Lohengrin or Mendelssohn's *Wedding March* from *A Midsummer Night's Dream*; indeed, millions of couples over the years would have felt the Sacrament of Matrimony somehow incomplete without them! All the same, there has emerged in recent years a snobbish cult of avoiding these hackneyed items at any cost. It is now regrettably fashionable to demand Widor's 'celebrated' *Toccata*—to my taste just short of musical vulgarity (in church, at any rate)—and technically unsuitable in the over-resonant surroundings of our lofty cathedrals and abbeys. Yet I well remember the great Charles Marie Widor improvising at *les Grandes Orgues* of St Sulpice, Paris, in a style almost Bach-like in its contrapuntal austerity. *En passant,* I was at the time equally privileged to hear Louis Vierne at Notre-Dame improvising *versets*—as is the French custom—to alternate verses of the psalms at Vespers in transcendingly beautiful and ingenious imagery of the psalmist's powerful narrative. I also heard Bonnet and Dallier at St Eustache and the Madeleine respectively; also Marcel Dupré and Marchal, both of whom I met on other occasions. The art of instant extemporization on a given theme seems to be as second nature to the French organists—rather like the Welsh propensity for compulsive vocal harmonisation—though I nurture an uncharitable suspicion that these eminent performers kept up their sleeves a store of generally serviceable episodic material to bridge the gaps between more pertinent manipulations of the submitted motif! Occasionally choir and organist would

131 The Fathers' private cemetery at Sydenham. Closed in 1952. 'The procession to the graveside went by way of a narrow downhill path – usually in pouring rain'. *(London Oratory album).*

accompany one of the Fathers on an 'away' mission for a wedding or funeral. These excursions were usually regarded as outings, especially by the boys. All too often, though, we would journey to Sydenham for the laying to rest of a deceased member of the Community. The grounds of the Fathers' country retreat contained a private cemetery. The procession to the graveside went by way of a narrow downhill path—usually in pouring rain. In addition to the specified Gregorian chant, we always concluded the Office with a reverent performance of Mendelssohn's *Beati Mortui.* Eventually the property was sold and a separate plot was allocated to the Fathers at Gunnersbury.

I have already indicated that I inherited a competent batch of choir-boys drawn largely from the Oratory Central School. I was told some parents would present their sons for audition ready-trained both vocally and instrumentally. Such treasures never came my way; and training eleven year-olds from scratch without Choir School facilities proved arduous to say the least. As time went by, leading choristers were produced who went on to achieve distinction in various walks of life, including opera and concert soloists of international repute, a pilot, an actor and even a cathedral director of music. They are too numerous to mention by name, but I take this opportunity of recording my gratitude to them for their outstanding service to the music of the Oratory over the years, and my pride in their subsequent personal triumphs.

From its commencement at Brompton, the Oratory singing has been the subject of unqualified praise. Would that I might have been present at the Solemn Dedication of the church in 1884; 'The *Te Deum* was sung by the choir to music composed expressly for the occasion by Mr Thomas Wingham, the director of the choir at the Oratory, which was

much admired. The music of the Mass was Beethoven in C; the Offer-
tory, *Regina Caeli* by H. Cherubini; the whole was admirably sung by
the Oratory choir with additional singers from other churches, number-
ing 150 voices, which accompanied [!] Mr Pitts at the organ in the first
movement of Schubert's Symphony in C as the procession left the
church.' I have quoted the above from a report by the correspondent of
*The Tablet* who attended the ceremony. Only once was the spell of such
heavenly music broken. It was during those early years when the choir
had to be disbanded through lack of funds. The situation was eventually
saved by the munificence of the Duchess of Argyll.

132 Thomas Wingham (1846-
1893). *(London Oratory album)*.

An article in *The Candid Friend* of April 1902 above the initials G. H.
(obviously *not* George Herbert, who contributed to Grove's *Dictionary of
Music and Musicians*) recounts his visit to the Oratory during Passiontide.
I quote: 'At Lent and Eastertide, the music at the Oratory is especially
beautiful; Lent, with the forecast of the Passion, has its *messes solennelles*
and its impressive chorales; Easter, with the joy-burst of the Resurrec-
tion, its glorious Masses and triumphal hymns. Both kinds of music are
finely rendered at the Oratory. It is the custom here to give the beautiful
compositions, so rarely heard, of Palestrina and his contemporaries
during Advent and Lent. During Passion Week, this music is to be heard
to perfection. On Palm Sunday, the interesting service, the Blessing of
the Palms, was given to music by Petts [sic] and Wingham, former
organists of the Oratory ...On Good Friday, Palestrina's "Reproaches"
were given. These were sung antiphonally by two choirs placed in
different parts of the building, the effect of such an arrangement being
very beautiful. On the evening of Good Friday an opportunity was
given of hearing Ermel's Mass [!]. This composition was found at Antwerp in manuscript and arranged by Wingham, to whose musical ability
and careful training the services owe so much. This is the only copy of
Ermel's music in this country, the Oratory being the only place in
England where it is produced. The *Gallia* was also sung. This is
Gounod's setting of the "Lamentations of Jeremiah", and especially
written by him as a lament for the sorrowing French nation after their
reverse in 1870. The music during Passiontide was sung unaccompanied,
as all such music should be and was, in every case, finely rendered by a
highly-trained and efficient choir. The correctness of tone and pitch, the
delicacy of the light and shade and, above all, the purity of the boys'
voices were remarkable. After many years' experience of various choirs,
and after hearing some of the best unaccompanied singing to be heard in
this country, I can say without hesitation I have seldom heard sacred
music sung in such a refined, artistic and reverent manner.'

Thomas Wingham, mentioned above in connection with the
Oratory's earliest musical records, was, unlike his immediate successors,
Barclay and D'Evry, adequately documented in Grove. The piece contributed by J. A. Fuller Maitland lists his numerous appointments and
includes a catalogue of an impressive number of compositions. Here it
may suffice to quote that he was born in 1846 and died in 1893; his first
appointment as organist was to St Michael's Mission Church at the age
of ten; that he was elected a Fellow of the R. A. M. and as early as 1864

133 Wilhelm Schultes. *(London Oratory album)*.

became organist at All Saints, Paddington. 'His church compositions are marked by suavity rather than austerity, and it is rather as a pioneer of better things in the music of the Roman Church than as a composer that his name will be remembered. He raised the services at the Oratory to a very high standard.'

On the other hand, all too little information is to be found concerning those shadowy figures, Pitts and Schulthes. In company with Wingham, they both left 'serviceable' choral items of which characteristic examples are quite properly retained to this day in the Oratory music lists. One thinks especially of Wingham's Vesper hymns; *Pangamus Nerio* for the feast of St Philip, and *Vexilla Regis* for Passiontide; Pitts' Palm Sunday antiphon *Hosanna Filio David* and the responsory *In Monte Oliveti*. Schulthes contributed the Gradual *Tenuisti* for Palm Sunday and the antiphons *Immutemur* and *Inter Vestibulum* and the Gradual *Miserere Mei Deus* for Ash Wesnesday. Who was Walter Austin whose stirring *Ingrediente Domino* still enlivens the re-entry procession on Palm Sunday? Could he have been an assistant organist or choirmaster, as was dear old Sinclair Mantell, who could always be called upon to play the organ, conduct the choir, or even compose music at a moment's notice? Mantell had been *répétiteur* at the Opera House, Covent Garden, for many years; and after the retirement of Barclay and D'Evry, remained on hand in the choir gallery until his dying day. He knew well—as we all in our turn discovered—that the Oratory church acoustics could be deceptive as well as flattering. Voices from the sanctuary sounded slightly flat in some corners of the choir gallery. Mantell admitted that he had deliberately trained the choirboys to sing a little sharp to compensate for the defect! The choir and organ at full blast *in situ* will sound distant or muffled in different parts of the building. The story goes that Fr John Talbot (1863-1939) once blew his nose stentoriously in the sanctuary and the choir responded: *Et cum spiritu tuo.*

At a time when Papal representations concerning musical propriety were being widely respected the Oratory musicians continued to specialise in the masterpieces of the Classical period. Not that they were defiantly wayward. Barclay's attempt to 'sanctify' Haydn has already been mentioned. But there is more than scant evidence to show that sweeping—if misguided—efforts were being made to conform to Papal authority so long as the classics were not to be abandoned. The Masses of Beethoven, Schubert, Cherubini and the rest were drastically dismembered. These great masters thought nothing of setting a single word to a whole page of musical re-iteration; or, having reached the half-way mark in a movement, of reverting to an earlier phrase of the text. Thus the prayers of the Ordinary of the Mass were often quite unintelligible to a devout worshipper. And so Barclay in London and Sewell in Birmingham altered the underlaying of the texts—not to mention the note values to match—and ruthlessly abridged these works so as not to hinder the action of the Holy Sacrifice of the Mass. Thanks to Fr Robert Eaton and H. N. Collins, the Oratorians of Edgbaston were many years ahead of Brompton; while not entirely forsaking Cherubini and his contemporaries, they nevertheless gave precedence to Palestrina-style and the stream of Pre-Reformation compositions Collins was tirelessly recovering.

It was during my early years at the Oratory that I embarked upon the publication of a definitive edition of Renaissance church music at the invitation of Mr R. D. Gibson, director of the well-known music publishing firm, J. & W. Chester Ltd. The venture was a continuation of the series *Latin Church Music of the Polyphonic Schools* initiated by my tutor, H. B. Collins, the most erudite of the Tudor music scholars of his day. I studied organ, piano and musicology with him for about eleven years as his constant and devoted companion. As Organist and Choirmaster at the Edgbaston Oratory he followed William Sewell, who had collaborated with Brompton's Arthur Barclay in an orchestral arrangement of Cherubini's *Mass in E* which was given a first hearing on Easter Sunday,

1902. Sewell, incidentally, left a wealth of splendid church compositions which are deserving of revival. I lost no time introducing to Brompton his elegantly flowing *Pangamus Nerio*—as a foil to Wingham's highly-esteemed—if flamboyant—setting of the same hymn for St Philip's Day. Although Collins trained the boys, Fr Robert Eaton, the Prefect of Music, invariably conducted the performances. I had always supposed the situation to be unique until I learned from a perusal of Fr Edward Bellasis' study of Cherubini that our own Fr Edmund Garnett (1845-1896) was for a time Choirmaster at Brompton. Collins was housed with the Fathers but also occupied a private studio in the adjoining Grammar School—a dusty book-lined apartment, where he would work in the early hours editing and collating his copies of manuscripts diligently transcribed in the libraries of Christ Church, Oxford; Peterhouse, Cambridge; St Michael's, Tenbury, and the British Museum. It was at Christ Church that he first guided my hand at the task of deciphering the notation of the treasures bequeathed to us by the Pre-Reformation English composers.

However, my main concern at the time was to clean up established favourites: Masses and Motets by Palestrina, Byrd, Victoria and the like. They were for the most part in print—or had been—but every fresh edition turned out to be a copy of the one before, perpetuating the same old errors of transcription, and postulating a most unsuitable under-laying of the verbal text. Work on Palestrina's *Missa Assumpta est Maria* took me to Rome to study a sixteenth century copy in the Vatican Library.

In an abounding age of broadcasting, the Oratory choir was already well established 'on the air' as a body of men and boy singers performing Latin church music programmes and religious services, not only from the Oratory church itself—which presented difficulties of a technical nature—but from the Little Oratory Chapel and many other outside venues. At first the Oratory Fathers agreed only reluctantly to broadcasting their choir, feeling—quite understandably—that outside activities might retard concentration on local obligations. But when they were eventually invited to contribute to the excellent BBC series 'Sermons in Stone', Fr Bevan went all out to accept the offer, with its evangelizing possibilities. Felix Felton was the enlightened producer, and Robert Speaight, the Catholic author and actor, was the eloquent narrator. The BBC Third programme in those days was under inspired directorship, as it continued to be with such distinguished figures as Sir Stuart Wilson and Sir William Glock, who were supported by a band of brilliant producers. The most notable and enduring of these figures of the Third Programme was Basil Lam, with whom I collaborated in researching and presenting a multitude of Early Music programmes, and to whom we must always be indebted for the formation of the *Schola Polyphonica*. It came about that the frequency of Oratory Choir broadcasts—which always required permission of the Fathers—and the increasing difficulty of the music required, was demanding more than our choirboys could undertake in addition to their Oratory commitments. Basil Lam suggested that I should supplement the choir with suitable adult female sopranos to speed up the preparation and performance of music that was going to demand a high degree of musical perception and execution.

And so, in 1947, I founded the *Schola Polyphonica*, a mixed choir of about twenty-four voices, which came to be regarded as an extension of the Oratory Choir. Its purpose was to provide an authoritative model for performing an unexplored source of mediaeval music of religious and historical significance. In addition to a core of Oratory male voices I enlisted a number of hand-picked sopranos with pure, clear, steady voices and mature musical development. Listeners to the *Schola Polyphonica* broadcasts, wrote often to say how much they admired the clarity of the *boys* voices!

And so it came about that the *HMV History of Music in Sound* was produced, covering the centuries from Pre-Gregorian Chant to the glorious masterpieces of the sixteeenth century. This important undertaking also was organised by Basil Lam. Some of the examples were provided by the Oratory choir of men and boys only; others by the newly-instituted *Schola Polyphonica*, embracing the cream of the Oratory male choristers. Then blossomed a long and rewarding epoch of Early Music broadcasting, Sacred and Secular; as I recall it, something like ten programmes per annum for years on end. I can record only a few of the composers that come to mind; Ockeghem, Josquin des Pres, Dufay, Fayrfax, Dunstable and so many more—Lassus, De Monte …For several years running we took part in the Promenade Concerts in the Albert Hall in the august presence of Sir Adrian Boult and Sir Malcolm Sargent, and within spiritual reach of our beloved Oratory round the corner. The Promenaders cheered and applauded our Palestrina, Byrd, Victoria and Lassus, no less than Beethoven and Tchaikowsky. We once gave an early work there to contrast with a similar setting by the Polish Penderecki; setting ancient against modern was a favourite device of Sir William Glock, who was then the presiding genius. I can recall two BBC studio broadcasts when we breathed the same air as Igor Stravinsky; once when we sang the fourteenth-century Mass of Guillaume de Machaut as a foil to Stravinsky's setting of the same text; and again when my boys were engaged to sing in his *Persephone*, when he heaped praises on them for their 'perfect contribution'. These boys were able to provide background music to innumerable film productions at Denham, Pinewood, Shepperton and other film studios around. In that way, there are many Oratory choirboys who still treasure the autographs of Lana Turner, Julie Andrews, Yehudi Menuhin, Victor Mature, Clark Gable, and many another.

When colour television was in its infancy, ITV—it may have then gone under a different name—put out a splendid feature entitled 'The Nativity'. Visually, it consisted of slow-panning camera shots of mediaeval altar-pieces by Breughel, Memling and Van der Goes. It was an exciting job timing and executing contemporary musical sequences to correspond with the visual unfolding of the Christmas story. The pictures and music were overlaid by the impressive voice of Cecil Day Lewis reading from the Gospel according to St Matthew. Kevin Smith, now a counter-tenor of international repute, but at that time a boy in the Oratory choir, sang beautiful treble solos. I think both Julian Bream and Desmond Dupré played their part in the instrumental accompaniment. Now that I have mentioned Kevin Smith, I must also let drop the name of a now famous tenor, Edgar Fleet, who started with me as a husky but devoted treble; who even now returns to the Oratory choir as often as worldwide engagements permit.

For a year or so after the war the Polish community in South-West London was given hospitality by the Oratory Fathers for a High Mass on Sundays and Holy Days. It was my privilege to act as *organista* on these occasions, and I was sad when they departed eventually to worship in their own newly-acquired church at Hammersmith. At 1 pm the Oratory church, which had already been filled several times over, was crowded again with a devout and fervent congregation. They brought their own splendid male-voice choir; and I came to know and love many of their enthusiastic choristers. The Polish Solemn Mass was always for me a joyous function, and I never failed to be uplifted by the exultant singing of the final National Hymn. Christmas came with its eagerly-awaited recital of some of the most beautiful Polish carols ever to be heard; *Triumfy, Lulaize, Jezunia* ...

As far as I remember, our own celebration of the Feast of the Nativity did not include any extended carol singing by the faithful, unless it was confined to the night services and the childrens' Mass on Christmas morning. I have a faint recollection that for a period 'The First Nowell' was entered into by all and sundry at the end of the morning High Mass. But a recital of Christmas music was given by the choir after Vespers on the Sunday within the Octave, and repeated on the Sunday following. Tickets were available for seats at Midnight Mass, but often enough hundreds failed to gain admission. I recall the solid queue of would-be

134 St Wilfrid's Hall. The recreation room of the Brothers of the Little Oratory. It was built in 1872 at the expense of Fr Sebastian Bowden. *(London Oratory album)*.

worshippers extending almost to Exhibition Road. Almost invariably we put on Gounod's *Messe des Orphéonistes*, while, during the protracted Communion of the faithful, a string orchestra provided by the renowned violinist, Marie Wilson, played soothing *Pastorales*, including Corelli's beautiful *Christmas Night*.

The Brotherhood of the Little Oratory has always been a powerful force in the life of the parish. As a band of Catholic laymen, practising the ideals of St Philip, the Brothers meet frequently for Spiritual Exercises in an indescribably beautiful and richly-furnished chapel. This Sanctuary, on account of its manageable acoustic properties, was destined to serve as a broadcasting studio for countless productions of Latin church music in days to come.

Any account of the Oratory music tradition—which has always been maintained by a corpus of the most gifted and dedicated musicians obtainable—would, nevertheless, be incomplete without reference to the part played by the Fathers themselves. One remembers with appreciation and affection a long line of Prefects of Music who smoothed the path of the professional music staff, in addition to sustaining the vocal demands of liturgical observance in the sanctuary. Fr Paul Connell (1901-1964) held this office for seventeen years in unbroken succession. He was a keen liturgist and a fastidious administrator, keeping one abreast of all solemnities and developments; and tendering occasionally his personal preferences in the choice of music—which one rarely found to be unacceptable. One of my best compositions for the Oratory was written to Fr Paul's meticulous prescription: a four-part setting of the *Te Deum*. It was required to alternate comfortably with verses of the Gregorian *Tonus Simplex* sung in the sanctuary; to be not over-polyphonic; rather taut and terse, and resembling in style the *Benedictus* canticle of Jacob Handl! The result was good enough to please Nadia Boulanger, the famous and fastidious teacher of music, whose maxims have influenced most of the leading musicians of our day, including Lennox Berkeley, Aaron Copland, Yehudi Menuhin and Clifford Curzon. Fr Clement Bevan, mentioned earlier in connection with my appointment, was my first Prefect of Music. I attended, more than once, his challenging evangelistic discourses at Speaker's Corner in Hyde Park.

All the successive Prefects of Music I was privileged to serve under: Frs Bevan, Matthews, Connell, Taylor, Wood, Bushell, and Addington, gave a good account of themselves vocally—though they might well have been assigned to that office for the possession of more appropriate attributes than a slender inclination to music.

Time was when the sound of music issued less often from the sanctuary, though the solemnisation of the liturgy always committed the Fathers to a considerable amount of vocal preoccupation. There were, for instance, the solo recitatives—sometimes protracted—for the Celebrant and attendant ministers. If too high-pitched a reciting-note were embarked upon for a lengthy Preface, all-round suffering could ensue! Also—as is customary in most religious establishments—the entire Community, old and young, the gifted and the less-favoured, were alike obliged to engage in the chanting of psalms, hymns and

135 Fr Paul Connell.

169

canticles when the Office was choral, as in the Holy Week liturgy and at Vespers on Sundays and Feast Days. The psalms were usually sung in verse-by-verse alternation with the choir in the gallery, though during Holy Week the chanting was more often confined to the sanctuary, where the older antiphonal custom was observed. The mental and physical stamina demanded in maintaining the initial pitch in psalm-singing is considerable, where age and maybe indifference are encountered in the choir. During these difficult years the so-called tone-deaf were making their presence felt. More than one of the Community was affected by this condition. (Tone-deafness is not explicitly defined in any dictionary or treatise—musical, medical or scientific—that has so far come to my notice.)

In willing obedience to the voice of authority I am persuaded that any remembered tributes to the Oratory's musical renown should be unreservedly included in a record of this kind. Appreciation and encouragement came in varying forms from many quarters. I can recall with satisfaction the frequent presence among the congregation of such notable figures as Sir Eugene Goossens, Sir Lennox Berkeley, Hilaire Belloc and his daughter-in-law, Stella. And so the chapels of St Joseph and the Seven Dolours came to be filled again with a new—and perhaps more discerning 'audience' than in the 'Good Old Days'. Morna Stuart, authoress and playwright, wife of Judge Nicholas, was received into the Church about that time. She introduced two music critics; William Glock of the *Observer*, and Jack Westrup of the *Monthly Musical Record*, who both rose to pinnacles of fame as time went by. Sir William became Head of Music at the BBC; and Sir Jack attained his avowed goal as Heather Professor of Music at the University of Oxford. Glock wrote enthusiastically of the Oratory music, and subsequently engaged me to give seven lectures on Polyphonic Music at his Bryanston Summer School of Music, in company with Jack Westrup, Nadia Boulanger and Paul Hindemith. While he was up at Oxford, Morna Stuart's brother, Fr Robert Stuart, had played a leading part in a production of Monteverdi's *L'Incoronazione di Poppea*. Here, at the Oratory, on the initiative of Fr Patrick Bushell, the Oratory Choir, augmented by a splendid consort of experts playing contemporary recorders, violi, cornetti and sackbuts, produced a memorable performance of the same master's *Vespers of 1610*. Many distinguished conductors and musicologists attended the event which was widely acclaimed as 'a momentous and enlightening realisation.' Ralph Vaughan Wiliams wrote to me often following my BBC Third Programme broadcasts, expressing deep interest in the Pre-Reformation Latin music I was bringing to light. When we eventually became acquainted at a meeting of the Plainsong and Mediaeval Music Society he thanked me warmly and repeatedly for 'revealing these early treasures'; adding that the *Schola Polyphonica* I had developed was the finest choral group he had ever heard. Whenever the Vienna Choir Boys sang in London, they traditionally attended the Solemn Mass on Sundays, decked out in their trim sailor uniforms. I was told they felt most at home in the Oratory.

Sir Lennox Berkeley wrote a *Mass for Four Voices*, which we sang at the Oratory. I was also responsible for its first broadcast performance on the Third Programme. Dr Edmund Rubbra of the Oxford Faculty of Music dedicated his *Mass for Three Voices* 'To Henry Washington and the Choir of Brompton Oratory.'

My thirty-six years attachment to the Brompton Oratory encompassed the greater and most rewarding part of my whole musical life. Now, having delved thus far into the past, I am conscious there is more that could be told; for with every dawn there springs a further flow of treasured memories. However, I have already covered my allotted space. And so, with the comforting reflection that the centenary of our church happily coincides with my own eightieth anniversary, I must bring to a close my record of a century of Oratory music: 'The playing of the merry organ, sweet singing in the choir', ever, at heart, conforming to the golden precept of St Gregory the Great: *'Non clamor sed amor cantat in aure Dei.'*

# THE ORGANS OF THE ORATORY

## *Ralph Downes*

Early in the afternoon of 13 March 1950, smoke was seen coming from under the door of the 'candle cupboard' near the Calvary Chapel in the church. The verger unfortunately opened the door, and the entire contents—hundreds of smouldering candles, as it turned out—burst into flame. Of course it was arson.

The fire quickly ate through the ceiling, the gallery floor above, and the nearest end of the organ. Under its saucer-dome, the loft became a roaring furnace; the intense heat even blistered the paint of the church's central cupola: some men working in the lantern came down like performing monkeys and smoke was soon seen issuing therefrom in the Brompton Road. Within minutes the Fire Brigade arrived and the threatened destruction of the whole building was providentially averted.

Inside, the thick black smoke obscured all the windows—it was pitch dark. When the air cleared and the environs of the organ had cooled enough to make approach possible, it was found to be a total wreck: what had not been burned or melted was ruined by the flood of water—the keyboards were a solid mass of swollen woodwork—and not another sound ever emerged from it.

Thus came to grief an instrument which when built in 1858 was, in London, second in size and importance only to that built for the Crystal Palace Exhibition (1851). It was part of a generous gift from Fr Faber's great admirer, the Duchess of Arygll, who had also saved the choral establishment from bankruptcy after the completion of the new house and the first church at Brompton in 1854. (The little organ brought from King William Street was quite inadequate for the larger building, and was now moved into the Little Oratory in the house, where it continued to give yeomen service for some years. It will be described later).

The specification of the new organ, built by Bishop & Starr, was: 4 manuals, C to a3, 58 notes: pedals C to e1, 29 notes.

Man. I: CHOIR

| | | | |
|---|---|---|---|
| Bourdon Bass | 16 | Piccolo (wood) | 2 |
| Sub Dulciana (from c) | 16 | Dulciana Mixture III | 1⅗ |
| Open Diapason (from c) | 8 | Bassoon Bass and Treble | 8 |
| Dulciana, Bass & Treble | 8 | Cremona (from c) | 8 |
| Stopped Bass | 8 | | |
| Metallic Flute (from c) | 8 | | |
| Viol di Gamba (from c) | 8 | | |
| Principal | 4 | | |
| Hohl Flute | 4 | | |
| German Flute (from c) | 4 | | |
| Fifteenth | 2 | | |

*Opposite page:*
136 The organ in the Oratory church. Designed by Ralph Downes, it was completed in 1954 after the destruction by fire of the previous instrument.

| Man. II: GREAT | | Man. III: SWELL | |
|---|---|---|---|
| Sub Open Diapason | 16 | Double Diapason, Bass & Treble | 16 |
| Open Diapason | 8 | Open Diapason | 8 |
| Bell Diapason | 8 | Stopped Clarionette Flute | 8 |
| Clarabella | 8 | Salicional | 8 |
| Harmonic Flute (from g) | 8 | Principal | 4 |
| Stopped Diapason | 8 | Keraulophon | 4 |
| Principal | 4 | Fifteenth | 2 |
| Wald Flute | 4 | Sesquialtera III | |
| Twelfth | 2⅔ | Mixture III | |
| Fifteenth | 2 | Contra Fagotto, Bass & Treble | 16 |
| Blockflute | 2 | Cornopean | 8 |
| Sesquialtera IV | | Hautboy | 8 |
| Mixture III | | Clarion | 4 |
| Posaune | 8 | | |
| Clarion | 4 | | |

| Man. IV: SOLO | | COUPLERS | |
|---|---|---|---|
| Flute Harmonique | 8 | IV/II, IV/III, III/II, I/II, III/I, IV/Ped, | |
| Tuba | 8 | III/Ped, II/Ped, I/Ped, Ped Superoctave | |
| Octave Tuba (prepared) | 4 | Tremulant | |

| PEDAL | | WIND PRESSURES | |
|---|---|---|---|
| Contra Open Diapason (prepared) | 32 | Great & Choir = 76 mm. | |
| Open Diapason (wood) | 16 | Swell = 89 mm. | |
| Open Diapason (metal) | 16 | Solo = 152 mm. | |
| Violone (wood) | 16 | Pedal = 76 and 127 mm. | |
| Bourdon (wood) | 16 | | |
| Principal | 8 | ACTION | |
| Stopped Flute | 8 | Mechanical and pneumatic lever. | |
| Fifteenth | 4 | | |
| Sesquialtera III | | | |
| Mixture II | | | |
| Bombardone | 16 | | |
| Clarion | 8 | | |

William Pitts, Fr Faber's young protégé and co-opted organist from the beginning, continued in this capacity successively under choirmasters Herr Wilhelm Schulthes and, from 1872, Thomas Wingham, during whose tenure the Oratory music attained a legendary excellence. But apart from the accompaniment of Masses and Motets by Haydn, Hummel, Schubert, Beethoven, Mozart, Cherubini etc., (occasionally with orchestra), the organ repertoire seems to have been neither worse nor better than was heard in Catholic churches elsewhere: typical solos were, March from *Die Zauberflöte,* a Nocturne by John Field, a 'Symphony' (which?) by Beethoven, and the banalities of Edouard Batiste from Paris.

During the building of Gribble's new church, the organ was put in store, and a new 3-manual one was loaned by Bishop & Son for use in the temporary iron church: it was subsequently sold to the Cathedral in Auckland, New Zealand, where it continued to function until quite recently.

When, the site being ready, the organ builders were instructed to reinstate the 1858 organ (enlarged by four new stops, including the

32-foot) in a new and greatly elevated gallery, it was clear that the architect had failed to allow sufficient room for it. (In the first church, the roof had actually been raised at the Duchess's expense, to take in the height required). The consequent congestion 'under an extinguisher' marked the first stage of its gradual, regrettable decline. Worse was to follow: the rebuilt mechanism gave trouble; there were various bickerings with the firm, and the atmosphere of dissatisfaction reached a climax in 1904 when J. W. Walker & Sons were commissioned to improve and maintain it.

The appointment of Arthur Barclay and Edward D'Evry, succeeding Wingham and Pitts in the early 1890s, established a new regime which had its impact on the organ. D'Evry, friend of the celebrated Edwin H. Lemare (composer of 'Moonlight and Roses') was an adherent of the latter's 'orchestral-transcriptionist' school of organ playing, and after the suppression of orchestras in church ordered in the papal Encyclical *Motu Proprio* (1903) he drifted easily into the rôle of 'one man band'. The Walker firm readily supplied him with rather incongruous quasi-orchestral *timbres*, partly discarding in their rebuilds of 1904, 1914 and 1924 much that was germane to the old organ's original tonal architecture especially in the Pedal division and thus it developed an unhappy dual personality—though it evidently did what the temperamental Barclay-Jones and the ingenious D'Evry required of it!

The Washington-Downes regime in 1936 inherited this very mixed bag of instrument and repertoire; and in view of our joint commitment to the lofty musical and liturgical ideals promulgated by the saintly Pius X, our growing dissatisfaction with the *status quo* was inevitable.

For my part, the dictates of musical purism indicated a gradual rejection of the orchestral view of the Oratory organ, and after Fr Paul

137 William Pitts. The first organist of the Oratory, who provided music for many of Faber's hymns. The exciting story of how he and his brother James ran away from their father at Elton to become Catholics is told in Ronald Chapman's *Father Faber*. *(London Oratory Album)*.

138 Edward D'Evry, who succeeded William Pits as organist of the Oratory. *(London Oratory Album)*.

Connell's appointment as Prefect of Music, I began a series of discreet operations, with his tacit encouragement, aimed at restoring the organ's original character.

With the advent of World War II, the Walker firm's activities were severely curtailed by government controls; and as Mr Reginald Davidson (Kingsgate Davidson & Co) was artistically refurbishing the organ in neighbouring Holy Trinity church, I obtained his assistance and his appointment. During the years 1944 to 1950, good progress was made and the effect of the old organ was considerably purified and ennobled.

The fire brought all this to a full-stop. Mr Davidson had neither the personnel nor the material resources to build a new instrument: and as by now Walker's were reconstructing the organ in Buckfast Abbey under my guidance, they were easily brought back on the Oratory scene.

Meanwhile, since 1948, I had been engaged in the designing of a monumental neo-classical organ for the Royal Festival Hall, as yet only partially built, and I welcomed the golden, unexpected opportunity of designing a completely new instrument, tailor-made for the Oratory. Particular attention had to be given to its capability for accompaniment of choir singers as well as large congregations, while safeguarding a traditional tonal architecture inherited from Europe as well as Britain, as a pioneering expression of the *Organ Reform* which had hardly reached these islands although it was making great headway in the USA. Its aims and objects were, briefly, the provision of clarified ensembles of pipes liberated from dungeon-like *organ-chambers*, speaking freely and naturally on very moderate pressures of air and encased in resonant tone-cabinets so as to project effectively in a large building: above all, *character* was always to be preferred to mere power.

Since the Oratory and the Festival Hall organs were thus breaking new ground they provoked an immediate storm of criticism from the Entrenched Establishment: but musicians, artists, architects and eventually the general public came to accept them and admire their tremendous versatility as musical instruments.

The new Oratory organ was finished in 1954, voiced by Dennis Thurlow and Walter Goodey under my guidance. The façade of the case was designed by Peter Goodridge ARIBA, supervising architect of the church.

Specification:
3 manuals, C to a3, 58 notes: pedals, C to g1, 32 notes.

| Man. I: CHOIR | | | |
|---|---|---|---|
| Gedackt | 8 | Scharf IV | ⅔ |
| Principal (prospect) | 4 | Cromorne | 8 |
| Rohrflöte | 4 | Tremulant | |
| Octave | 2 | | |
| Waldflöte | 2 | | |
| Larigot | 1⅓ | | |
| Sesquialtera II | 1⅓/2⅔ | | |

| Man. II: GREAT | | Man. III: SWELL | |
|---|---|---|---|
| Quintadena | 16 | Barpijp (conical) | 8 |
| Principal (prospect) | 8 | Quintadena | 8 |
| Rohrflöte | 8 | Viola | 8 |
| Octave | 4 | Celeste (from A) | 8 |
| Gemshorn | 4 | Principal | 4 |
| Quint | 2⅔ | Gedacktflöte | 4 |
| Superoctave | 2 | Nazard (conical) | 2⅔ |
| Tertian II | 1⅓/1 3/5 | Octave | 2 |
| Mixture IV-V | 1⅓ | Gemshorn | 2 |
| Trumpet | 8 | Tierce | 1 3/5 |
| | | Mixture IV | 1 |
| | | Cymbel III | 1/5 |
| PEDAL | | Echo Trumpet | 8 |
| Principal (prospect) | 16 | Vox humana | 8 |
| Sub Bass (wood) | 16 | Tremulant | |
| Quintflöte | 10⅔ | | |
| Octave (prospect) | 8 | | |
| Gedackt | 8 | COUPLERS | |
| Rohrquint | 5⅓ | III/II, I/II, III/I, II octave-grave. | |
| Superoctave | 4 | III/Ped, II/Ped, I/Ped. | |
| Nachthorn | 2 | | |
| Mixture IV | 2⅔ | WIND PRESSURES | |
| Bombarde | 16 | Great = 78 mm. | |
| Trumpet (extension) | 8 | Choir = 66 mm. | |
| Trumpet | 2 | Swell = 70 mm. | |
| | | Pedal = 91 mm. | |

ACTION
electro-pnematic, with mechanical swell-pedal.

The small organ built for King William Street in 1849-50 by Gray & Davison had the following specification:
2 manuals: Great, C to f3, 54 notes: Swell to c to f3, 42 notes: Pedals C to d, 27 notes.

| Man. I: GREAT | | Man. II: SWELL | |
|---|---|---|---|
| Open Diapason | 8 | Double Diapason | 16 |
| Keraulophon (from c) | 8 | Open Diapason | 8 |
| Clarionet Flute (from c) | 8 | Stopped Diapason | 8 |
| Stopped Bass | 8 | Principal | 4 |
| Principal | 4 | Fifteenth | 2 |
| Flute (from c) | 4 | Cornopean | 8 |
| Fifteenth | 2 | | |
| Sesquialtera ?III | | | |

ACTION
Mechanical and probably partly pneumatic.

PEDAL
Grand Bourdon                16

COUPLERS
II/I, I/Ped, II/Ped.

139 Ralph Downes in 1982.

When the Community moved to Brompton, this organ was first put into a 'west' (i.e., *south*) gallery in the temporary church (1853-54): but in 1855 it was decided to make a Lady Chapel cum organ–alcove in a shallow transept near the sanctuary on the Epistle side, and the gallery was taken down. With the arrival of the large new organ the Bishop firm moved the small one into a new gallery at the west end of the Little Oratory chapel in the house.

In 1872 this chapel was entirely refurnished (as now) and the organ was rebuilt according to the taste of the time by Brindley & Foster of Sheffield and moved into a chamber behind a rather pleasant (but 'dummy') Italianate façade, in a tribune above and behind the altar. The new specification was:

2 manuals, C to c4, 61 notes: pedals C to f1,30 notes.

Man. I: GREAT

| | |
|---|---|
| Bourdon (wood, part old) | 16 |
| Open Diapason (old treble) | 8 |
| Hohlflöte (wood) | ·8 |
| Lieblich Gedackt (wood, old) | 8 |
| Dulciana (old treble) | 8 |
| Zartflöte (wood, part old) | 4 |

Man. II: SWELL

| | |
|---|---|
| Geigenprincipal (old treble) | 8 |
| Rohrgedackt (sic!) (part old) | 8 |
| Viola da Gamba | 8 |
| Voix Celeste (from c) | 8 |
| Salicet (old treble) | 4 |
| Horn | 8 |

PEDAL

| | |
|---|---|
| Sub Bass | 16 |
| Bourdon (from Great) | 16 |
| Flute (independent) | 8 |

COUPLERS

II/I, I/Ped, II/Ped, II octave, II suboctave.
Tremulant to whole organ.

WIND PRESSURE

±90 mm (later raised to about 100 mm).

ACTION

The builder's patent tubular-pneumatic
(sliderless).

140 The Little Oratory organ, built to the design of Ralph Downes in 1975.

A century later, an anonymous donor enabled it to be replaced in 1975, worn out as it now was, by a worthier new instrument, built *into* the façade (now filled with fine tin pipes) by the Dutch firm D. A. Flentrop (Zaandam): the specification, layout and finishing were approved by me, on the same aesthetic principles as applied to the new organ in the church. The resonant case occupies only the thickness of the arch surrounding it; thus although soft, the tone is better projected into the whole chapel than was its louder predecessor. The large 'organ-chamber' is now empty.

Specification:

2 manuals, C to g3, 56 notes: pedals, C to g1, 32 notes.

| Man. I: GREAT | | PEDAL | |
|---|---|---|---|
| Prestant (from G) (in front) | 8 | Subbas (wood) | 16 |
| Roerfluit | 8 | Bourdon (metal) | 8 |
| Octaaf | 4 | Octaaf (in front) | 4 |
| Fluit (stopped) | 4 | Fagot (cylindrical) | 16 |
| Gemshoorn (wide, conical) | 2 | | |
| Mixtuur III-IV | 1⅓ | COUPLERS | |
| Kromhoorn | 8 | II/I, I/Ped, II/Ped. | |
| Tremulant | | | |
| | | WIND PRESSURE | |
| Man. II: SWELL ('Bovenwerk') | | 62 mm. | |
| Gedekt | 8 | | |
| Roerfluit | 4 | ACTION | |
| Prestant | 2 | Pure mechanical, the upper manual | |
| Nasard (wide, conical) | 1⅓ | suspended. | |
| Sesquialter II | ⅔/1⅓/2⅔ | | |
| Tremulant | | | |

# APPENDIX

## LIST OF PROVOSTS OF THE LONDON ORATORY

| | |
|---|---|
| **1850** | Father Wilfrid Faber |
| **1853** | Father Wilfrid Faber |
| **1856** | Father Wilfrid Faber |
| **1859** | Father Wilfrid Faber |
| **1862** | Father Wilfrid Faber |
| **1863** | Father Bernard Dalgairns |
| **1865** | Father Father Francis Knox |
| **1868** | Father Philip Gordon |
| **1871** | Father Richard Stanton |
| **1874** | Father Richard Stanton |
| **1877** | Father Stephen Keogh |
| **1880** | Father Philip Gordon |
| **1883** | Father Philip Gordon |
| **1886** | Father Philip Gordon |
| **1889** | Father Sebastian Bowden |
| **1892** | Father Philip Gordon |
| **1895** | Father Ignatius Antrobus |
| **1898** | Father Philip Gordon |
| **1901** | Father Ignatius Antrobus |
| **1904** | Father Sebastian Bowden |
| **1907** | Father Henry Cator |
| **1910** | Father Henry Cator |
| **1913** | Father Henry Cator |
| **1916** | Father Edward Crewse |
| **1919** | Father Edward Crewse |
| **1922** | Father Edward Crewse |
| **1925** | Father Ralph Kerr |
| **1928** | Father Ralph Kerr |
| **1931** | Father Wilfrid Burnham |
| **1934** | Father Father William Munster |
| **1937★** | Father William Munster |
| **1945** | Father William Munster |
| **1948** | Father William Munster |
| **1951** | Father William Munster |
| **1954** | Father William Munster |
| **1957** | Father William Munster |
| **1960** | Father Juvenal Matthews |
| **1963** | Father Juvenal Matthews |
| **1966** | Father Edward Leicester |
| **1969** | Father Michael Napier |
| **1972** | Father Michael Napier |
| **1975** | Father Michael Napier |
| **1978** | Father Michael Napier |
| **1981** | Father Charles Dilke |
| **1984** | Father Charles Dilke |

★Owing to the war the triennial election which should have been held in 1940 was postponed until 1945.

# Index